"The authors of this brilliant expositi‹ ‹no ordinary academics, although acad‹ more faculty scholars such as these. They are also master organizers, part of a network of Native and other community organizers in Indian Country fueling the process of decolonization of Native lands and communities. Bordertown violence is as old as US colonization of the continent itself, and it persists today in the towns and cities that border Native reservations and communities all over US-claimed territory and is replicated in even more distant cities that have large Native populations, many of whom are homeless. This may be the most important organizing manual ever produced by a social movement in the United States."
—Roxanne Dunbar-Ortiz, author of *An Indigenous Peoples' History of the United States* (Beacon Press, 2014)

"The borders racking our world are in constant motion and, like the explosive grinding of tectonic plates, the violence of this movement and resistance to it emerges most sharply at the edges. This essential volume brings together militant intellectuals to provide an accessible introduction to the violent encirclement of Native communities and to provide crucial concept weapons to deepen ongoing collective resistance."
—George Ciccariello-Maher, author of *Decolonizing Dialectics* (Duke University Press, 2017)

"*Red Nation Rising* shines a revolutionary spotlight on border politics in the United States. By centering the framework of bordertown violence, this book extends and sharpens our critical understanding of what it means to struggle for liberation and freedom on stolen land. Showcasing the ways that settler colonialism works through our ideas about place, belonging, migration, and territory, the book's crucial theoretical interventions and anticolonial manifesto demand that we think differently about what constitutes 'the border.' Essential reading for academics and political organizers committed to radical praxis and politicized solidarity with everyday Native people resisting colonial occupation."
—Jaskiran Dhillon, associate professor of global studies and anthropology, the New School, author of *Prairie Rising: Indigenous Youth, Decolonization, and the Politics of Intervention* (University of Toronto Press, 2017), coeditor of *Standing with Standing Rock: Voices from the #NoDAPL Movement* (University of Minnesota Press, 2019)

"A remarkable body of work that effectively weaves long overdue native scholarship and historical analysis of settler colonialism with direct and timely frontline reports on the continuing bordertown wars and conflicts in occupied native territories. Offers a comprehensive framework for advancing present and future indigenous resistance and liberation struggles."
—John Redhouse (Diné)

Red Nation Rising

From Bordertown Violence
to Native Liberation

Nick Estes, Melanie K. Yazzie,
Jennifer Nez Denetdale, and David Correia

Red Nation Rising: From Bordertown Violence to Native Liberation
© 2021 Nick Estes, Melanie K. Yazzie, Jennifer Nez Denetdale, and David Correia
This edition © 2021 PM Press

ISBN: 978–1–62963–831–7 (paperback)
ISBN: 978–1–62963–906–2 (hardcover)
ISBN: 978–1–62963–847–8 (ebook)

Library of Congress Control Number: 2020934728

Cover by John Yates / www.stealworks.com
Interior design by briandesign
Cover Photo by Sandra Yellowhorse

10 9 8 7 6 5 4 3 2

PM Press
PO Box 23912
Oakland, CA 94623
www.pmpress.org

Printed in the USA.

Contents

Foreword

Radmilla Cody and Brandon Benallie

Prior to European contact, the area currently known as Albuquerque, New Mexico, was considered neutral territory by various Native societies located near the grand river flowing through it. Native people nourished by the river regularly met in the area to trade food, items (ceremonial, cultural, and practical), songs, and stories. It was an area of mutually agreed upon peace for the sake of kinship.

On July 19, 2014, two unsheltered Diné (Navajo) men named Kee Thompson and Allison Gorman were asleep on a soiled mattress in an empty lot when they were targeted by three teenagers continuing an old settler tradition called "Indian rolling." Gorman and Thompson were savagely murdered, beaten beyond recognition. Although Albuquerque police stated the murders of Gorman and Thompson were not motivated by race, the grim implication was there, as it always has been since first contact with European settlers in this hemisphere. A few days later, a news reporter with the Associated Press interviewed the lone survivor, Jerome Eskeets, who was sleeping nearby when Gorman and Thompson were attacked. The video interview shows Eskeets crouching in the passenger seat of the reporter's car, bruised, shocked, and in fear for his life. He keeps his head low, retelling the story of what happened to the men he called his "uncles," pausing a few times to quietly sob. As he recounts the jeers of "homeless" that the teenagers yelled as they beat Gorman and Thompson, Eskeets finally turns his head toward the reporter's camera and says, "We're not homeless. Our home is right here on this land."[1]

The cosmic weight of these murders pulled together many fierce relatives, guiding seemingly distant paths of liberation into their own river of commitment to action. However, this is not another collection of stories about the tragedy of settler and Native relations. *Red Nation Rising* is the continuation of what we, as Diné, would call *k'é hasin*: everlasting kinship and hope. We enacted kinship as we sought justice for Gorman and Thompson and all unsheltered relatives on the front lines of the war against colonialism. Through kinship, we build solidarity and commitment to liberation for the Earth's poor, displaced, and dispossessed people. Through kinship, we are strong.

Radical relationality is not a new idea, nor is it an "indigenized" theory of kinship, just as theories of mutual aid and dialectical materialism are not European inventions. Kinship and critical thinking have always been part of the foundations of Native lifeways, providing balance in our collective journey. There is now a monstrous disruption in the balance of all relatives who live above and below the surface of the Earth. Today, in our era of life, this monster is known as capitalism, the most threatening and successful force of death and poverty.

We must remind ourselves that borders on this hemisphere are recent lines drawn by the claws of capitalism. Borders preserve an imbalance, favoring those who benefit from the misery of broken kinship. Capitalism's insatiable hunger for violence is manifested by every border structure it builds. The suffering and indignity Palestinian people experience when crossing an Israeli checkpoint is similar to that of Yaqui people held at gunpoint by US border patrol agents, with the same company providing walls and surveillance technology for both borders.

How often have we heard from apologists for capitalism that this is the most peaceful time in history? Peaceful for whom? When the United States embarked on a new enterprise called treaty-making, they made sure to include promises of peace. History has proven the peace promised in treaties was never meant for Native people. Settlers militarized the borders drawn up during the treaty process with outposts we know today as bordertowns. These outposts, primitive bordertowns, were meant not only to contain "off the reservation" Indians, but to prevent Black relatives and other enslaved human beings from seeking refuge within Native societies.

Towns in general are designed by and for men; they are literal structures of patriarchy. There are more streets, towns, and landmarks named after dinosaurs than named after women. Bordertowns are sustained through the use of the four B's: the bullet, the bottle, the bank, and the

Bible. Bordertowns base their identity on the historical myth of the Wild West, a free market capitalist utopia for those seeking to fulfill an ultra-masculine, gunslinging fantasy. Anything that interferes with this fantasy is immediately eliminated, no matter how reasonable the appeal to reality is. And this reality is the immiseration and exploitation of Native lives, lands, and intelligence.

The bordertown is a reflection of every symbolic gesture made toward Native people to pacify currents of rebellion. Predatory lenders from payday loans to pawnshops ensure a constant stream of debt flows through capitalism's maw. Vampires exist in bordertowns; they drain the life embedded within Native art and culture. Devoid of spirit, they are an insult to death itself. Every day we bargain with the beast so that we may buy groceries for the week, so that we are not pulled over by cops in the dark or followed home to where our children sleep. The time for bargaining is over.

As Diné, we continue to pray to Monster Slayer and Child Born of Water. We are comforted by Grandfather Fire, a direct connection to the cosmic flame: *Nitsáhákees* (critical thinking). We sing songs of rebellion and hope. We sing songs about monsters who were slain, because they brought illnesses to the mind and body. The songs are woven in a borderless blend of strategy and victory. They remind us of the strength of kinship necessary to defeat ancient enemies who have returned once again.

Our roots of resistance are strong and smooth as grandmother's hands, burying our hearts deep within the Earth. These humble roots will always seek nourishment from those who remember the Beauty Way songs of their people. These roots are beyond borders and will always find you. They will always find you.

The Earth and Sky gave us all unique tools and abilities to slay the monster known as capitalism. This book is one of them.

CHAPTER ONE

"I Can't Fucking Breathe!"

Twenty-nine-year-old Zachary Bearheels, a citizen of the Rosebud Sioux Tribe, needed to see his mother. He left his aunt's house on the Rosebud Reservation, where he'd been staying, and boarded a Greyhound bus in Murdo, South Dakota, on June 3, 2017, bound for his mom's home in Oklahoma City. He never reached her. The bus pulled into Omaha, Nebraska, late on a Saturday night, June 3, 2017. Bearheels, like most passengers, got off the bus to look for food or maybe a clean bathroom. While he was gone, another passenger complained to the driver that Bearheels was strange, his behavior erratic. The driver refused to let him back on the bus when he returned.

Bearheels suffered from bipolar disorder and schizoaffective disorder and required anti-psychotic medication to control his symptoms and stay well. He'd run out of the medication, and his symptoms returned. Abandoned in Omaha, without money or medication, Bearheels spent the night walking across the unfamiliar city. He walked past two of its hospitals and dozens of its churches. He walked past the Joslyn Art Museum, famous for its Native-themed architecture and its collections chronicling European conquest in North America. When the bus arrived in Oklahoma City without him, Bearheels's mother, Renita Chalepah, filed a missing person's report.

Bearheels walked all day and into the next. Sometime after midnight on June 5, he made it to a gas station and convenience store miles from where he'd started, exhausted, dehydrated, and hallucinating. A store clerk found him licking the windows of the store and dancing on the sidewalk in the dark. The clerk called the police, and two cops arrived, Jennifer Strudl and Makayla Mead. They handcuffed Bearheels and placed him in the back of Strudl's cruiser. They ran a record check and saw he'd been reported missing. Strudl called Bearheels's mother at 1:00 a.m. Chalapeh was up, so worried about her son that she hadn't slept at all. She explained to Strudl that she was ready to drive to Omaha but needed to know her son was somewhere safe. He didn't have his medication, she said, and he needed help. "Please bring him somewhere safe," she pleaded, and suggested a crisis center, if possible. Strudl radioed her supervisor, Sergeant Erik Forehead, who refused Chalapeh's request. "Take him back to the bus station," he ordered.

Just then another cop, Scotty Payne, arrived. He pulled into the convenience store lot just as Strudl was opening the cruiser door to talk to Bearheels. But Bearheels was having none of it. He slipped past her and out of the cruiser, his hands still cuffed behind his back. The three officers chased after him. A fourth cop, Ryan McClarty, arrived, just as the others grabbed Bearheels and pinned him against a bottled water display on the sidewalk outside the store.

Some of this we know from lapel camera video, but all of what follows was captured by a camera in Strudl's cruiser. The officers briefly release Bearheels, who turns away from them and stands facing the store. The four cops discuss something off camera, and then suddenly Strudl appears in the frame, walking toward Bearheels. She turns him around, back toward the cruiser and then the other cops join her, putting hands on Bearheels. The video is grainy but Bearheels looks confused and quickly grows alarmed. McClarty grabs Bearheels roughly by his ponytail, while another officer pushes him toward the cruiser. Bearheels isn't fighting back, but he struggles to get their hands off of him. As they approach the open cruiser door, walking toward the camera, Bearheels drops to the ground, his hands still cuffed behind his back. The officers circle him. Scotty Payne yells, "Taser! Taser!" and fires at Bearheels. The violent jolt of electricity knocks Bearheels onto his back. Only his legs and torso are visible. He lays momentarily still, breathing heavily, gasping for air. What looks like convulsions begin, but it's more likely the electricity coursing through his body.

Most Tasers that police carry can be used in one of two ways. On drive stun mode, an officer presses the Taser directly into a person's body, delivering the electrical potential of 50,000 volts. Payne, however, fires the Taser like a gun, launching electrically charged darts toward Bearheels. The darts are attached to the Taser by wires and they attach to their victim like the fangs of a snake. In this mode, a cop can deliver the pain of electrocution over and over again. Bearheels lies on the ground as Payne cycles the Taser, twelve times in all, electrocuting Bearheels repeatedly over the course of nearly sixty seconds. The maker of the Taser, Axon, claims it is a nonlethal weapon, but this is true only if police use it as a nonlethal weapon. They don't. Police kill dozens of people with Tasers every year.

Payne stands over Bearheels holding the Taser, pulling the trigger every few seconds. Bearheels writhes on the ground, kicking at him with his unlaced, high-top sneakers. It's unclear if Bearheels is trying to fight Payne off or simply convulsing from being electrocuted. Suddenly, McClarty lunges toward Bearheels and grabs him again by the hair. He lifts him off the ground and slams him down, driving his body into the pavement. "You're gonna get it again," Payne hollers. In the violence of the attack, Bearheels slips his cuffs and his right hand comes free. He frantically tries to defend himself against McClarty, but the cop spins him onto his back and pins him to the pavement. With his left hand McClarty holds Bearheels down, and with his right he unleashes a flurry of punches to Bearheels's head. These are vicious punches, shocking in their force and efficiency. McClarty throws thirteen punches in eight seconds, each directly to the head. Each punch sends Bearheels's head snapping back onto the pavement. Punch, pavement, repeat.

The other three officers stand over Bearheels, watching—and doing nothing—as McClarty kills Bearheels. A woman's cries are heard in the background. Bearheels says, "I can't fucking breathe!" and then goes limp. The other officers continue to throw Bearheels around while Payne radios for a rescue squad. The police place cuffs on Bearheels's limp arms and put flex cuffs on legs no longer kicking. Paramedics arrive. They find no pulse. He is not breathing. They bring him to a hospital, one that he'd walked past just hours earlier, where doctors pronounce him dead.

The coroner's report determines that Bearheels died from excited delirium syndrome, despite the fact that there is no such thing as excited delirium syndrome. Neither the American Medical Association nor the American Psychiatric Association recognize it as a legitimate medical condition. It is a euphemism that coroners use for people that police kill with their tasers or in chokeholds.

Omaha police chief Todd Schmaderer fires Payne, McClarty, Strudl, and Mead. Payne and McClarty are charged with assault, but a jury acquits

Payne, and prosecutors later drop misdemeanor assault charges on McClarty. Police "experts" convince the prosecutors that McClarty was justified in punching Bearheels. When Bearheels slipped his cuffs, they explain, he posed a threat, and McClarty was justified in eliminating that threat. Apparently handcuffs, that most common of carceral tools, are a lethal weapon when not in the hands of cops. In April 2020, an arbitration panel upholds Payne's termination but reinstates McClarty, along with Strudl and Mead. They receive back pay but are required to take a "refresher" course in policing.

"I Can't Breathe"

A month later, in May 2020, after three of these four cops—now Indian killers—are reinstated as officers, four Minneapolis cops murder George Floyd. There is no flurry of punches, as with Bearheels. Derek Chauvin pressed his knee into the back of George Floyd's neck. One cop tells Chauvin, "I'm worried about excited delirium or whatever." He asks if they should turn Floyd on his side. "That's why we have him on his stomach," Chauvin responds. "I can't breathe," gasps Floyd. Like with Bearheels, all of this is captured on video, and millions of people eventually watch as police slowly choke the life from Floyd while he cries out for his mother.

As in Bearheels's case, the initial medical examiner's report says nothing about police violence. "No physical findings support a diagnosis of traumatic asphyxia or strangulation," the first report read. It is "underlying health conditions" not the racial animus and white supremacy at the heart of American policing that killed Floyd. Is this the definition of excited delirium? The slow grinding down of the bodies, hearts, and minds of Native, Black, Brown, and poor people by police?

It is not enough to say that police killed Bearheels or Floyd, nor is it enough to focus on the particular sadism of Payne, McClarty, and Chauvin. Rather, our task is to ask how we might account for their deaths, understood as a product of a murderous system built on Native extermination and anti-Blackness, a system designed to lead directly to premature Native and Black deaths. This is the quotidian nature of white supremacy—the everydayness of genocide—and it reaches deep into Native and Black lives, breaking hearts, shattering minds, and destroying bodies. These are the preexisting conditions for millions.

The murder of George Floyd sparked ferocious, organized, and principled movements for Black lives in a historical force unseen in generations. Countless many have tirelessly organized for years against police and the murderous system of white supremacy police uphold and defend. They were ready for this moment, because this moment is every moment. Millions took to the streets to direct righteous anger at the institution of policing itself. The aftershocks of these seismic ruptures toppled monuments of Confederate generals, Spanish conquistadors, and racist sports mascots. Decolonization and abolition are not mutually exclusive.

Elites and nearly all elected officials, as expected, have scoffed at or patronized these Black and Native-led uprisings, condemning and vilifying those taking to the streets. "Why do people burn down their own neighborhoods?" they ask. Because these have never been *their* neighborhoods. US cities have never *belonged* to Black people. The end of chattel slavery offered no end to white supremacy. The plantation system continued on in the form of Jim Crow and in a ruthlessly policed racial apartheid organized around the theft of Black wealth. Black people were no longer the property of white overlords, but race relations—between Black and white—have always been—and remain—a property relation. Police are the enforcers of this relation, patrolling Black people as the plantation overseers once did, making, upholding, and defending racialized property relations. The geography of the United States is a geography of white supremacy—the Jim Crow sundown towns and the property redlining that reinforced it—a geography of unfreedom that excludes Black people from owning homes and land and of possessing collective social wealth.

It is this history that kindled the fires that erupted in cities throughout the United States following the murder of George Floyd. You can't burn down your "own neighborhood" if it never belonged to you. It belonged to police, so we set it on fire. What burned was not Black property, but white property, the property of the owning classes: their chain stores, payday loan centers, fast-food chains, slumlord buildings, and banks. By burning down the police stations that patrol the plantation, people burned down the plantation. The fires burned brick and mortar, but the target was a different form of property, what the legal scholar Cheryl Harris called "whiteness as property."[1] Whiteness is not a thing but a property relation based on an exclusion ruthlessly enforced by the state. How could it be anything other in the United States than the social and spatial expression of a homicidal settler worldview constructed through cultural, legal, and political norms of extermination and genocide? The masses in the streets

5

broke the spell of inviolability surrounding the plantation to teach us that whiteness burns too.

From the Plantation to the Bordertown

The plantation is where capital was first amassed from the forced labor of enslaved African people on the stolen lands of Native people. Expropriating wealth based on forced labor and stolen land requires an astonishing commitment to collective colonial violence. This commitment fueled US westward expansion. The settlers dragged the relations of the plantation along with them as they raped and murdered their way through Native lands. It took more than temporary settler outposts to sustain this commitment to violence, and so these outputs developed into towns and cities. This is what settlers meant when they talked of bringing "civilization," as they liked to say, to *their* "western frontier."

We call all of this the *bordertown*. Settler colonialism has so transformed the world we live in that few settlers see their cities as spatial expressions of settler violence. The word instead took on other meanings. The bordertown most commonly describes the cities and towns along *recognized* international borders, such as the US-Mexico border. These are considered the borders that matter in the everyday life of a settler. We draw on Native vernacular, an everyday language of resistance, to recognize the borders that settlers ignore. These borders exist everywhere settler order confronts Native order. And since we find this confrontation everywhere in settler society, everything in a settler world is a border, and every settler is haunted by this border—a Native presence that should not exist, that blurs the edges of settler ontology. This fundamental contradiction compels settlers to act like settlers; they sense the threat but cannot name it; they are always on the defensive.

The bordertown typically refers to white-dominated settlements that ring Indian reservations and give spatial form to the violence and exploitation that defines everyday Native life, past and present. The bordertown is a cruel invention that imposes on Native people a million daily indignities. The bordertown, however, is not just a place. It is a relation where the contradictions of settler colonialism emerge and show themselves to all. The constant crossing of borders is everywhere. The spatial transitions of off- and on-reservation, the moving across international boundaries, the skipping into and out of jurisdictions, and the knowledge that every Native step constitutes a transgression of a settler border and a settler rule.

"Off the reservation" is a political and military expression designating someone who is uncontrollable and, therefore, a threat to power. "Originally the term [*off the reservation*] meant a particular kind of 'outlaw' a Native person who crossed the territorial border, called a reserve or reservation, set by the United States or state government," writes the Laguna Pueblo feminist Paula Gunn Allen.[2] The reservation, more prison than homeland, offers no refuge from this settler geography. According to Gunn Allen, the boundaries also include imposed political and heteronormative norms, the strictly enforced divisions of territory, race, gender, and nation. A transgression of these cruel fictions—"going off the reservation"—made one a renegade, an outlaw, who could be hunted down and, usually, executed. Many reservations began as prisoner of war or concentration camps—and some remain so. Settler law *allows* Native peoples to call these homelands, but only until settler law says they can't.

Like all property, the bordertown is many things at once. It is a thing and a relation, a place and a project. As a project, it is cunning in its capacity to make Native peoples appear foreign in their own lands. The Native is always *out of place* in the bordertown. The aim of this book is not to offer a cultural, or even geographical, analysis of the bordertown. Rather, we seek an analytical precision for the category, a category that we believe is crucial in the struggle for Native liberation. This term is our term, because it is the term that Native people themselves use. Its multiple meanings describe not only a place but also an experience. *Red Nation Rising*, therefore, makes no contribution to scholarly studies of colonialism. Ours is an elaboration of a collective Native experience of struggle against colonialism. The bordertown only exists to eliminate the Native, and to steal and secure Native land.

Language, of course, does matter, as the common practice among coroners of renaming police murder "excited delirium" makes clear. Everything found on Turtle Island, for example, has a Native name. Many are known by several names, a result of overlapping, negotiated relations among Native peoples to specific places. These names persist despite the violence of settlers who destroy these places and, by virtue of their "discovery," rename them, often after an Indian killer or slaver. We note the increasingly common gesture among some non-Native people to refer to places by their Native names. We encourage the proliferation of Native languages and the restoration of Native place names. But renaming places by their Native names does not restore land to Native people, just as rejecting the language of excited delirium does not bring Zachary Bearheels back to life. The bordertown serves the settler no matter what we call it.

We use the term *bordertown* to keep the focus on its origins and purposes and the relations that it sustains. This is the analytical precision we seek. The word *bordertown* also captures a very specific accusation. The name itself—a noun, *town*, adjectively modified by *border*—reveals and clarifies the settler project. Every town is a bordertown, because every town serves as a border that settlers must defend. But the name *bordertown* anticipates its own failure and predicts its own demise. This is why we render it as one word. It is a bordertown, not a border town. Why? There is no objectively innocent spatial form in a settler world that we might call *just* a "town." Rather there is only the spatial expression of the settler project—borders, violence, and police. Every settler town is a bordertown, because every Native person on land that the settler desires, whether in a city or on the reservation, represents and embodies the active ongoing failure of the settler project. *Bordertown* is the word that describes the murderous colonial condition that has come to structure Native life and, thus, Native resistance to overturn that order. The only way to resolve this fundamental contradiction is through Native liberation.

The Upside-Down Places

Bordertowns, as with all imperial borders, are spatial expressions of an intent to murder. This is why, from Saskatoon to Santa Fe, bordertowns are always bloody killing fields. Omaha and Minneapolis, two bordertowns whose settler names are taken from the languages of the Native nations from whom they were stolen, are united by a settler violence so deeply embedded in everyday life as to achieve a kind of banality in its regularity. It is so common, this violence, that it seems to disappear into the air that the settler breathes.

Omaha and Minneapolis, like all bordertowns, were carved from what settlers called "the frontier." You find the frontier, according to the historian Frederick Jackson Turner, at "the meeting point between savagery and civilization."[3] Consider the phrase. In the speech Turner gave during the 1893 World Columbian Exposition in Chicago titled "The Significance of the Frontier in American History," his "meeting point" served as a metaphor to describe a United States finally and fully emerged.

In other words, this place the settler calls the United States cannot exist outside the settler domination of Native lands. Another word for *meeting point* is *bordertown*, where the settler confronted and sought to destroy a Native world in order to *become* the United States, in order to individually become "American."

Police use the exact same language. Police call the "meeting point" the thin blue line between two antagonistic social worlds. Like Turner, police understand the meeting point as the line between civilization and savagery. The thin blue line updates Turner's frontier thesis. For Turner, the meeting point served as a metaphor to describe an event—the conquest of Native lands. The thin blue line makes clear that this was no event. It is an ongoing practice. Thus, the United States requires genocidal violence as long as a Native world persists. Police use the thin blue line to remind us that this *imperial* project is a police project. Without police, or without the settler, there would be no *United States*. So settlers and their police occupy these "meeting places," the Omahas and Minneapolises, the wellsprings of the United States and progress, these upside-down places. They are upside-down for the way the bordertown makes police violence look like self-defense and a defense of civilization necessary to protect settlers from the savage threat of Native retribution.

Settlers Need Indian Killers
The settler is always white. The bordertown is always under attack. The Native must always be destroyed. This is the recipe for an always present settler fear and anxiety stoked by the terror of a coming "great replacement" fantasy, a "white genocide" in which Native and Black people are in constant rebellion, always threatening to do to the settler what the settler did first. To the settler, the only reasonable response to this is violence. Destroy the Native before the Native destroys you.

Police are settler society's Indian killers. McClarty, Payne, and those Omaha cops killed Zachary Bearheels for embodying this existential threat, as did Derek Chauvin. George Floyd is not the only man he killed. In 2006, Chauvin and other police shot Wayne Reyes, a citizen of the Leech Lake Band of Ojibwe, twenty-three times, killing him. Police awarded Chauvin a medal of valor for his Indian killing, as they always do.

Trace the work of the cop back in time. The first frontier police in the United States were the scalp hunters recruited into Indian Country to murder Apaches in the 1840s and 1850s. Chauvin and McClarty are their descendants, a product of a long line of scalp hunters, mutilators, and body part collectors. Churches in Santa Fe once ran the scalps of Apaches up their flag poles. In Minnesota, settlers collected scalp bounties on Dakota men, women, and children. Frontier newspapers advertised land for sale alongside rewards for bloody "red skins." The violence of the settler has always been understood as productive, progressive, and, thus, lawful. Police create order out of this imagined chaos.

These scalp hunters never left, never fully gave way to police. Instead, they exist alongside them as de facto police. In April of 1974, three white high school students from Farmington, New Mexico, murdered three Navajo men, Benjamin Benally, John Harvey, and David Ignacio. The teenagers bludgeoned their faces and caved in their chests with basketball-sized rocks. They exploded firecrackers in their noses and on their genitalia. They burned and beat their victims beyond recognition.

The Chokecherry Massacre, as it came to be known, is standard police and vigilante practice. There is nothing unusual about this brutality, particularly in Farmington where white high school students have been known to sever the fingers of Navajo people living on the streets and display them proudly in their lockers at school. Murdering and torturing Navajo people in the bordertowns that surround the reservation has its own name: *Indian rolling.* These are the scalp hunters of their generation.

The practice of Indian rolling is bound up in a state-sanctioned death culture practiced mostly by white male settlers. Winslow, Arizona, police officer Austin Shipley worshipped killing. He once posted a selfie wearing a III% skull t-shirt in his squad car. These men are hunters, and policing has always followed the logic of the hunt. The cop hunts when on patrol. On March 27, 2016, Shipley received a call about a woman shoplifting at a Circle K gas station and convenience store. The clerk claimed a woman stole two cases of beer and a gas station hotdog. Shipley hunted her, and the point of the settler hunt is the kill.

He pulls up behind Loreal Tsingine, a twenty-seven-year-old Navajo woman, a young mother, walking down the sidewalk. Shipley fumbles with his lapel camera, tries to turn it off, in fact, but all this does is deactivate the audio recording function. So, from his own lapel camera we watch his hunt without sound. He leaps from his cruiser, grabs Tsingine from behind, shoving the hundred-pound woman so forcefully to the ground that the sidewalk tears flesh from her arm as she falls. She shows no fear as she recovers from the blow and turns to face her attacker, raising a pair of blunt-ended forceps in defense. Shipley fires at her four times at close range. She falls and Shipley stands over her calmly watching her die, gasping for air.

Among the items Shipley carried with him on his hunts was a Punisher skull patch, the common insignia of police, military, and settler militias. The patch represents the masculine heart of the settler's commitment to the hunt. The settler forges his masculinity in violence against Native women. The cop and the vigilante are represented by the Punisher logo, both versions of the same "anti-hero engaged in a war against evil, seemingly without end." These are the words the creator of the comic book uses to explain the Punisher. "God will judge our enemies, we'll arrange the meeting." This phrase adorned the range bag Shipley placed alongside him when he took his police cruiser out for his hunts. The settler understands the hunt as a divine mission to kill.

Off the Reservation

Settler citizenship entails a lethal obligation to kill Indians. And the history of settler colonialism is a history of the professionalization of this obligation. The settler hired the Indian killer to cleanse the land and make way for white settlement. The settler got the world, the Indian got the reservation. It is from this history that the common American English idiom "off the reservation" comes to us, with all its genocidal meaning. For the settler, the obligation to "cleanse" territory of any Native presence and claim it is the first premise of collective violence. From this premise comes perpetual violence, extermination, and the drive to erase all that is Native. More dead Indians, more settler land. The Indian killer had counterparts in the east who were slave patrollers hunting, capturing, and returning enslaved Africans to plantation overseers.

But Native people and Black people are not hapless victims. There is a reason the thousands of protests that erupted following the murder of George Floyd were described in mainstream media as an "uprising." There is nothing that terrifies a settler more than the words *Indian uprising* or *slave uprising*. In fact, the founding document of the United States, the Declaration of Independence, mentions Native and Black people in the same paragraph, citing "domestic [slave] rebellions" and "the merciless Indian Savages" as two major threats facing the nascent settler nation.

These are our histories of resistance. Consider the Dakota Uprising of 1862, when the Dakotas, enraged by constant abuse at the hands of white settlers and broken treaties, burned down trade forts and attacked colonial settlements. Draw a straight line between the Dakota uprising and the burning of the Third Precinct in Minneapolis. Connecting these two reminds us of our shared struggle, but it also reminds us to prepare for the backlash, because settler backlash always follows an uprising. Settlers imprisoned and hanged the Dakota patriots in 1862 for their crime of wanting freedom. In 1863, a white settler captured and scalped the Dakota leader of the uprising, Taoyateduta (also known as Little Crow). A mob dragged his body through the bordertown of Hutchinson, while white children exploded firecrackers in his nose and mouth. This was how they celebrated their Fourth of July.

Native activists founded the American Indian Movement (AIM) in Minneapolis in 1968, inspired by the Black Panther Party for Self-Defense. Like the Panthers, they came together to protect their relatives from police who constantly beat Natives for being "off the reservation." All law is settler law, so self-defense is always a crime when practiced by Native or Black people. Police and vigilantes killed AIM and Red Power activists as retribution. The FBI waged a terror campaign through its notorious COINTELPRO program.

We keep drawing this line and it passes through Gallup, New Mexico, where two young Navajo men, Larry Casuse and Robert Nakaidinae, kidnapped Mayor Emmet Garcia in 1973. Garcia embodied the anti-Indianism at the heart of Gallup. In addition to being mayor, he was a co-owner of the Navajo Inn, the most profitable liquor establishment in the state of New Mexico at the time, perched along a lonely highway between Gallup and the Navajo Nation. Like all bordertowns, Gallup was, and remains, a machine that settlers built to kill Native people. It was, in Casuse's and Nakaidinae's time (and very much still in ours), an economy organized around the exploitation of Native people: check cashing, payday lending, pawning, high interest auto lending, liquor sales, and bars. All of these existed—and still exist—to target Navajo people, who had, and continue to have, few alternatives on the reservation.

If you wanted to see bordertown violence, you went a few miles off the Navajo reservation to the Navajo Inn, where vigilantes killed Navajo men and women, and then dumped them in ditches alongside the road. The most common cause, according to the coroner, was "death from hypothermia," but, like excited delirium, this was a euphemism. Most died violent deaths at the hands of vigilantes or police. In a two-year period in the late 1960s, vigilantes and police killed twenty people and injured ninety-one more along a sixteen-mile stretch of road that connects the Navajo Inn to the Navajo Nation. Many of those were within a mile of the Navajo Inn. Thirty-six people died of alcohol-related "accidents" in one three-year period in the 1970s.

Without police, the bordertown as we know it would not exist. Gallup police made, on average, eight hundred public drunkenness arrests each month in the early 1970s. Police waited in the parking lots of liquor stores and along the alleys behind local bars, hauling people to jail night after night, hunting. Nearly every person they arrested was Navajo. They held these men and women in what at the time was the largest county jail in the United States, an overcrowded and decrepit "drunk tank." They hunted; Native people hid.

But Casuse and Nakaidinae did not hide. They resisted. These were the material conditions in Gallup that led Casuse and Nakaidinae to kidnap the mayor at gunpoint, parading him down Gallup streets. They barricaded themselves in a sporting goods store on Route 66. State police sharpshooters took up positions on rooftops along the street.

Robert put down his weapon to build barricades against police, and Garcia, his hands cuffed behind his back, kicked him away and dashed for the front door. Garcia came crashing through the front window, glass flying. Police sharpshooters opened fire; the barrage of bullets and chemical munitions sent onlookers scrambling for cover. Robert burst out of the store and through the gas, his hands high in the air, his voice pleading for help for Larry, who was lying face down in the back of the store, covered in blood. Police dragged Larry's body onto the street where cops, one-by-one and in groups, took turns posing in front of his body, smiling, holding rifles. Like any proud hunter, they took pictures of themselves with their kill.

Larry Casuse committed the ultimate crime against settler law. He refused it. He rejected colonial arguments that blamed Native people and instead understood the problem as one inherent to the political economy and policing of the bordertown. The problem was not that Navajo men and women were drinking in Garcia's bar; it was that they were dying. He saw it in the liquor stores and bars and on the streets of Gallup. Despite the doctors and public health officials of the time who blamed "Indian drinking" on genetic or cultural deficiencies among Native people, Casuse asked who and what killed them. When he answered the question—settlers—he acted, entering into a long tradition of radical Native resistance. In the death of Larry Casuse, just as in the deaths of Zachary Bearheels, Loreal Tsinignine, and also George Floyd, the logic of the bordertown reveals its lethal obligation: kill the Indian, save the land. And build a fort to defend settler society.

The settler is right to be afraid, because the Native is, in fact, coming for his fort. The Native will kidnap his mayor. The Native does have plans to burn his police stations to the ground. A Native world will grow from the ashes of his settler world. A Native world is under constant erasure but always on the verge of return. The settler is right to be afraid. Natives oppose the law precisely because they uphold a different kind of order, one that opposes the settler's commitment and obligation to collective violence. This is the settler past, present, and future: perpetual fear.

In September 2016, The Red Nation, a Native-led revolutionary organization, organized a Larry Casuse Spirit Ride from Albuquerque to Standing Rock to bring supplies to Water Protectors camped on Dakota and Lakota land and fighting to stop the construction of the Dakota Access Pipeline. By then, Water Protectors had been standing their ground for more than four months against National Guard units and nearly a hundred different law enforcement jurisdictions. The Minneapolis Police Department was one of many jurisdictions on the ground. Police attacked, maimed, and arrested Water Protectors, deeming them "insurgents" on the Great Plains. Like Zachary Bearheels, their crime was being on their own land and, as with Larry Casuse, settler police attacked them for their refusal to accept a settler world.

From Larry Casuse to The Red Nation

In the early morning hours of July 19, 2014, three teenagers entered a dirt lot on Albuquerque's Westside. The teens had spent the night wandering back alleys looking for homeless men to beat. For months, in gangs of three and sometimes more, they hunted mostly Native homeless men in a blood sport of violent beatings. On this morning, they found three Navajo men in a vacant lot sleeping on mattresses. Not cops armed with truncheons and Tasers, the teens gathered broken cinder blocks and caved in the heads of two of the men, Allison Gorman and Kee Thompson. After the cinderblocks, they hit them with metal poles. Leaving the scene long enough to retrieve knives from their homes, the teens returned and stabbed Gorman and Thompson in the heart.

Gorman, from Shiprock, New Mexico, and Thompson, from Church Rock, New Mexico, were Diné. Jerome Eskeets, also Diné, miraculously survived the attack. The boys had done this before, he would later explain. He told the *New York Times* that these same teens had threatened him with an attack earlier in the month, but he did not report the threats, "because no one cares."[4] After their arrest, the teens, the oldest eighteen and the youngest fifteen, admitted to beating Native men living on the streets frequently, estimating as many as fifty prior attacks within a year.

These attacks brought the Navajo Nation Human Rights Commission to Albuquerque in December 2014. The commission held a public hearing at the Albuquerque Indian Center, a place where unsheltered Native people get a free lunch, connect with social services, and pick up their mail. The mayor of Albuquerque refused to attend the hearing, perhaps fearful he might be kidnapped. The director of the commission opened the hearing by explaining that the investigation would focus on vigilantism but also on police. "The role of the police is supposed to be to protect and serve," he explained, "but our people tell us that we need to protect ourselves from the police."

One after another, Native people testified about the constant violence of police. "I was the Indian, so I was the bad guy, I guess," one explained. "The police aren't going to help us. They don't care." Another explained that police harassment of unsheltered Native people "happens whether we're homeless or not. The danger is everywhere. But the homeless are just easier targets. Someone was shot to death on the streets recently, and no one even heard about it. It wasn't reported."

To be Indian in public, to walk the streets of bordertowns, is a transgression of the anti-Indian common sense that permeates settler society. As those who testified all knew, like Casuse and Nakaidinaie before them, to be Indian in the bordertown is to be a problem that needs solving. To be Indian in the bordertown is to remind settlers and their Indian killers that you are not extinct, that you claim the humanity and the rightful relations with the lands they arrogantly claim as their own. It's also to be poor and often without a house. Of the estimated twenty-five thousand Native people living in Albuquerque, 13 percent are chronically houseless like Gorman and Thompson. Many live in a part of Albuquerque that police call the "War Zone." According to the unsheltered Native people who live in that part of town, the war being waged is by police against Native people.

After listening to the testimony at the Albuquerque Indian Center, we walked through the War Zone to hear the stories of Native relatives on the streets. We met a man a few blocks from the Albuquerque Indian Center who told us he's constantly harassed by police, "You know, I'm an alcoholic, and I drink on the streets, and [the police] picked me up, and they brought me all the way down to the [zoo], and they beat me up while I was in handcuffs, and then they unhandcuffed me and let me go." The practice of apprehending Native people on the streets and dropping them off miles away from their encampments is a common tactic of settler police. Like Zachary Bearheels, this man walked through a city hostile to his presence, past its hospitals and schools and wealthy homes, only to be terrorized by Albuquerque police who hunt Native people as part of their mandate.

A few blocks away, we met another man who told us, "I was walking on the street, and [a cop] was following me. I'd go down the alley, and he'd follow me. 'Why don't you go back to the rez. You're not welcome here in Albuquerque,' he told us." We met a Jicarilla Apache man named Natani at a tent camp who had had the same experience. "This is ours, our land," he said. "And the cops, they'll say things like 'Why do you want to bring the reservation our way?'" We asked him how often police harassment includes physical violence. He gave us an impatient look. "It's usually," he said. He showed us his wrists, covered in scabbed-over wounds. These were from handcuffs, he said. He pulled off his sunglasses to show a red and swollen eye. "They maced me in this eye. They walked up to me from behind and maced me like this," he said, as he put his hand inches from his eyes to show us how it was done. "How common is this? Does this happen to everyone?" we asked. "Yes," he said. "They handcuff you, and then they beat you, and then they take you to the hospital and say something like 'We found him this way.'"

Days later, we met two women walking near the Albuquerque Indian Center. One woman told the story of a cop who had recently slammed her head to the pavement. "Then he just got back in his car and drove away." The other woman described constant harassment. "They pull up and tell us to leave or they'll arrest us for loitering," she said. "Where does this happen?" we asked. "Everywhere," she said.

We write this book as part of The Red Nation. The Red Nation began in the summer of 2014, in Albuquerque, New Mexico, on the heels of Gorman's and Thompson's murders. Like Casuse and countless others before us, we could no longer stay silent about the gruesome Indian rolling happening every day around us. The anti–police violence uprising of spring 2014, which ignited after Albuquerque police gunned down a man named James Boyd in the foothills east of the city, was winding down, and the United States was on the precipice of experiencing a Native intifada the very next year, with uprisings in Oak Flat, Mauna Kea, and Standing Rock in quick succession. The conditions were ripe for Native liberation.

The Red Nation belongs to the traditions of Native resistance like AIM and Red Power that were born in bordertowns. Like these earlier generations, we seek to destroy the place *and* the relation of the bordertown. Our name comes from a Lakota term—*Oyate Luta*—which describes "the Red Nation"; humble people from the red earth, the Native of the Western hemisphere. From Rapid City to New York City, all will be again The Red Nation when we liberate the bordertown and replace settler colonialism with freedom.

This book, *Red Nation Rising: From Bordertown Violence to Native Liberation*, offers a guide to the world that settler colonialism has made through bordertowns. Our goal is not to understand the bordertown but, rather, like Casuse, to map its weaknesses so we can burn it to the ground. We refuse its logic. Reject the history it tells. But how does a book refuse its subject? We are reminded of an apocryphal story of the Bedonkohe Apache warrior Goyathlay, also known as Geronimo. It is said that Goyathlay had magical powers. He could summon rainstorms and slow the passing of time. He could occupy two places at once and could fight two enemies simultaneously. The settlers and their armies would give his name—Geronimo—to all of their subsequent fears. Everything that had to die for settler colonialism to live, they named Geronimo. The act of merely being alive, of refusing to surrender or submit, of refusing even to fear those who hunted him, terrified settlers. They murdered his mother, his wife, and his children. They sent nearly half the US Army after him. They captured him, and he escaped. Captured again, he escaped again.

Of all the supernatural powers credited to Goyathlay, perhaps the most astonishing—the one from which all settler fears are derived—was his refusal to accept the settler world. What other than some supernatural power could explain Goyathlay's refusal in the face of a murderous settler world spreading like a plague over Apache lands?

Through this refusal, Goyathlay conjured a different world than the one the settlers had made. He lived as one who belonged to a different world. The burning of a police station in Minneapolis or Portland and the toppling of an Oñate conquistador statue in Albuquerque is such a refusal. Should we live in a world organized around Native and Black death, or should we refuse this world, burn it to the ground, and conjure another in its place? We contend that the Native world of Goyathlay may be forgotten by some, but it never left, just as we have never left.

We have organized this book as a map of the bordertown rendered in textual form, organized by the concepts that animate the settler world, and those that conjure its opposite. We offer short essays, including "Anti-Indian Common Sense," "Church," "Tourism," "Savage," Poverty," "Bordertown Political Economy," "Vigilantism," and "Police Violence," among others. These are all simultaneously places and concepts, things and practices. They give the bordertown its form and function. We have mapped them so you will know where to find them—and where to set the fires of Native liberation. Among these concepts we also offer essays that define the world that will replace the world of the settler—"Abolition," "Decolonization," "Kinship," "Solidarity," "Liberation," "Sovereignty," and more. These constitute hidden (and sometimes not-so-hidden) geographies of Native resistance that will grow from the ashes of the settler world.

We write as ancestors from the future, enacting just relations that cannot be found in the nightmarish present of the bordertown. In this sense, the settler fears the future. He is an alien in both space and time. This book offers no measured gestures toward liberation, nor mercy for settler feelings. The word for that is *reform*. But the bordertown cannot be reformed and settler society cannot be redeemed. We study it not to change it but to destroy it. To read this book is to move back and forth between the settler world and the Native world, to enter into relations of liberation that can replace the bordertown. The Native liberation we write about is not some distant dream from some future world.

Our history is the future.

CHAPTER TWO

Anti-Indianism

Anti-Indian Common Sense

Anti-Indian common sense combines what Dakota scholar Elizabeth Cook-Lynn calls "anti-Indianism" with what Italian Marxist revolutionary Antonio Gramsci calls "common sense." North American settler societies are organized around the elimination of the Native. Therefore, anti-Indian common sense is the ideology that organizes Native elimination, encompassing everyday racist depictions of Natives in popular culture (like mascots) and more spectacular forms of genocidal violence (like massacres).

In *Anti-Indianism in Modern America*, Cook-Lynn defines anti-Indianism as the broad array of views that result in or carry out the death, elimination, and genocide of Natives. This includes the writing of history and literature that deliberately ignores Native existence, nationhood, and sovereignty, that denigrates or insults being Native, or that blames Natives for an unsatisfactory history. Anti-Indianism is how settler society expresses itself through both law and culture. The settler state and its institutions—police, courts, prisons, schools, hospitals, nonprofits, the military—create the law, but everyday settler citizens carry it out. "All of these traits," Cook-Lynn writes, "have conspired to isolate, to expunge or expel, to menace, to defame" Native people of North America.[1] Anti-Indianism is foundational to North American settler colonialism.

For settler societies, to ignore anti-Indianism is to participate in it. In his *Prison Notebooks*, Gramsci uses common sense to understand how spontaneous consent is achieved in Western capitalist societies. For Gramsci, common sense refers to "the conception of the world which is uncritically absorbed by the various social and cultural environments in which the moral individuality of the average man [*sic*] is developed."[2] While common sense encompasses individually held beliefs, it is a structured belief system that governs society and partitions the planet along racial and class lines.

Gramsci understood common sense as upholding the capitalist exploitation of workers. Workers have to internalize or consent to ruling-class ideology to keep the system going. Settler colonialism, however, does not require consent from Natives nor does it necessarily have to be internalized by Native people themselves. If consent is required, it is often achieved through coercion or force: assimilation, starvation, neglect, imprisonment, or the cooptation of Native leadership. While working-class consent to capitalism is sometimes achieved through force, it is not in capitalists' best interests to kill off the entire working class, whose labor they need to exploit to make profit. While the settler ruling class does not require consent from Native people, it does require consent from the settler working class to uphold the larger structure of settler capitalism that serves ruling-class interests. This is where anti-Indian common sense comes in. Settler citizens and vigilantes are conscripted into anti-Indian common sense to carry out the sacred duty of land dispossession and capitalist accumulation. And they are typically not coerced or forced but see their everyday obligation to carry out the project of Native elimination as a part of their identity as settler citizens. Settler citizenship and vigilantism, conditioned on many obligations, are also consummated through Indian killing. Together, anti-Indianism and common sense describe the structure of violence at work in settler capitalist societies like the United States and Canada.

Off the Reservation

Off the reservation is a common American English idiom. According to the Oxford English Dictionary, *off the reservation* means "to deviate from what is expected or customary; to behave unexpectedly or independently." The expression is also common in US military and political circles. Someone who goes off the reservation has gone rogue or vigilante, disobeying orders: a soldier "crosses the wire" of a military base (called a *reservation* in military lingo) without leave or enters into hostile territory (called *Indian Country* in military lingo) without orders.

For Native people, to go off the reservation refers to those who refuse reservation life. The usage of the phrase *off the reservation* derives from the nineteenth-century Indian wars of extermination, reservation imprisonment, and the genocidal violence waged against those refusing to respect imperial borders. Like the military bases that share the same name, Indian reservations are militarized spaces of containment, meant to control Native movement and behavior. Indian reservations were designed as concentration camps to facilitate Native elimination by removing them from desired lands. Reservations were never meant to be "homelands," though, for some, they have become that today. In the past, Natives who willfully crossed reservation borders were renegades, outlaws, or hostiles, who were hunted down, shot, lynched, executed, scalped, or imprisoned.

Bordertown spaces are designated as off the reservation, where Native life is heavily policed and controlled. Since a majority of Native people in North America today do not live "on the reservation," their reality is defined as living life off the reservation. In this way, to live life off the reservation is a historical question of territory and a political practice—a direct challenge to where and how Native life and sovereignty ought to exist—or not. Cops and everyday settler citizens frequently tell Native people, "Go back to the reservation!" as a way to assert settler claims to land and Native unbelonging, when the reality is the reverse. According to Kahnawà:ke Mohawk scholar Audra Simpson, the trespass of the Native into what is considered "settled" territory and a "settled" history calls into question the finality of Native elimination and dispossession.[3] The continued existence of Natives on desired lands, especially in bordertowns, calls into question the entire settler colonial project.

Territory, whether on or off reservation, is, Patrick Wolfe argues, "settler colonialism's specific, irreducible element."[4] The erasure and elimination of the Native, therefore, is not based on race, blood quantum, culture, religion, worldview, or spirituality—it is simply to gain access to land. Once Native territory is acquired, it does not become an inactive element. It requires continual *doing*—an anti-Indian common sense that performs ownership and belonging at the expense of Natives. The continued presence of Natives in "settled" territory presents a special problem for that *doing*—a problem that has throughout history been called the "Indian Problem."

Defining space as on or off reservation concedes that Native territory and land is permanently settled and that territory will be forever defined according to imperial borders.

Indian Country

It is no coincidence the US military refers to all enemy territory as "Indian Country," sometimes shortened to just "In Country." According to the Oxford English Dictionary, *Indian Country* in American English designates "a land or territory controlled or inhabited by American Indians" and "a place with hostile inhabitants, a dangerous area." These two definitions of territory might appear different but are better understood as synonymous.

Indian Country is a military term that designates enemy territory and identifies the Indian as the original enemy of US empire. It was in Indian Country at the Battle of Wabash, in 1791, that Little Turtle of the Miami and Blue Jacket of the Shawnees annihilated the regular Army under the command of "Revolutionary War" hero Arthur St. Clair. Next to the destruction of Custer's Seventh Cavalry at the Battle of Little Bighorn by Lakota, Cheyenne, and Arapaho warriors—a battle that came just weeks before the one hundredth anniversary of the signing of the Declaration of Independence—the Battle of Wabash, also known as the Battle of a Thousand Slain, was the most devastating defeat of the US military in American history.

Native nations, along with freed Black forces, allied with the British against the American colonists during the revolutionary war to oppose US independence, which depended on colonial expansion into the Ohio River Valley and the expansion of slavery. In other words, for Black and Native people, the US war for independence was little more than a counterrevolutionary war of settler territorial expansion. After the Battle of Wabash, with the entire US standing army crushed, Native nations reclaimed the Ohio River Valley. This was the historical context of the Second Amendment. The right to bear arms has never been about some abstract notion of "freedom." Rather, it has always been about settler colonial anxiety and insecurity. With its standing army destroyed, white male settlers were organized and armed into "well-regulated" militias to prevent the return of the British and their allies, Native nations and freed Black forces. Thus, the reversion of "settled" land to its original free state—Indian Country—is the ultimate fear.

For this reason, US empire finds itself in Indian Country wherever it finds a threat to imperial authority. As Chickasaw scholar Jodi Byrd argues, "the United States propagates empire not through frontiers but through the production of a paradigmatic Indianness" that it finds everywhere.[5]

Indians are the original Red Scare, and enemies of empire are always made Indian, whether in Vietnam, Iraq, Afghanistan, or anywhere else the US has boots on the ground, in any of the eight hundred US military bases across the globe.

Every US war is an imperialist war, and all are an extension of the Indian Wars. And each of these wars includes its own Geronimo. Geronimo, known as Goyathlay, led the longest insurgency against the United States (1850–1886), evading capture and refusing confinement, forever "off the reservation." This is why Geronimo has become a ubiquitous feature of US military authority terrorizing the world. Paratroopers jump from airplanes into enemy territory, or Indian Country, shouting "Geronimo!" Osama bin Laden, a CIA-funded jihadist, was given the code name Geronimo. To be in Indian Country is to be forever in enemy territory.

Drunk Indian

A Facebook post appears on my feed: "Drunk Indigenous people are still sacred and deserving of community." This seemingly innocuous post delves into a history of Native peoples and their introduction to alcohol, first by settlers, and then by their government representatives, who facilitated the theft of Native lands with alcohol. Europeans, and then Americans, brought alcohol as a trade item and plied Native leaders with drink to facilitate treaties to acquire land, natural resources, and material items, such as pelts and clothing, as well as to exploit human labor. Incoming settlers and army soldiers were notorious for their drunken bouts, encouraging Native peoples to model their behavior and relationship with alcohol. Because alcohol use has been the source of dysfunction and violence in Native nations and communities, Indians, already cast as inferior and savage, are further demonized simply because they drink alcohol.

One of the most racist images of Native peoples is that of the "drunk Indian." It is used to excuse society's behavior toward Native people who live on the streets of bordertowns. It is presumed that these individuals are the dregs of society who deserve hatred, discrimination, murder, and rape, because they are already not human. Racist stereotypes about "drunk Indians" have resonance in bordertowns, where liquor sold to Native peoples is profit-making. Bordertowns are death spaces for Native peoples cast endlessly as "drunk Indians." Deemed as less than animals,

Native people like Raymond Yellow Thunder, Allison Gorman, and Kee Thompson, among countless others, are viciously mutilated, tortured, and murdered. However, as the script that begins this entry indicates, Native peoples have always demanded that Native forms of kinship extend to those who face some of the deepest structural forms of disparity and injustices, of which widespread alcoholism is but a symptom. Recognizing that the trope of "drunk Indian" is deployed in a host of ways to excuse violence by settler nations is an important step toward Native liberation.

Over generations, self-proclaimed Indian experts have ventured to bordertowns to find the reason for what seems to be rampant drunkenness among Native people. These experts use all the tools of universities, nonprofits, and policy think tanks to argue that the Indian is morally deficient, because he can't hold his drink. An oft-cited study by the Indian Health Service in the mid-1980s determined that, on average, Indians die more frequently of alcohol-related causes than non-Indians. They conclude that Indians are "tragic," because they have not been able to adjust to a modern world. The trope of the Indian stuck between two worlds emerged from these studies. As expertise in Indian victimization grew into an entire industry of trauma-informed research, researchers "discovered" that Native alcoholism is the result of genetic predisposition to addiction. Native people cannot overcome alcoholism, these experts explain, because violence is so pervasive in Native life that it now predetermines their genes. While researchers continue to acknowledge the disproportionately high rates of alcohol-related deaths among Native people, it would be inaccurate to say that alcoholism is entirely the result of genetic trauma. Alcohol abuse is a condition created by colonial systems of oppression that forces Native peoples to leave their homes and communities and seek survival in hostile bordertowns. Alcoholism is a colonial technology that can only be dismantled by decolonization.

Urban Indian

The term *urban Indian* automatically invokes layers of meaning that reify stagnant notions of the "Indian" in which a binary of "traditional"/"urban" and "rez"/"city" becomes the truth about what it means to be a Native person in the current moment. This binary becomes a barometer for who is "more authentic" or "more traditional," with those who reside on designated "reservations" or Native nations seen as somehow more rooted in cultures and traditions associated with ancestors and those who reside in "urban" environments or the "city" seen as more assimilated and, therefore, less rooted in the cultures and traditions of their nations. Reservation spaces are simultaneously cast as places of poverty/stagnation and cultural/traditional resurgence, whereas the city is cast as a place of opportunity/progress and as assimilated/modern. Such labeling reinforces settler colonial notions of who is Native, with the caveat that Native peoples uncritically deploy these categories in their own judgements of one another.

These binaries are ahistorical and stagnant, because their meanings are rooted in late nineteenth-century salvage ethnography, the same era in which famed anthropologist Lewis Henry Morgan, who we discuss in our entry on kinship, birthed modern ethnography by studying the supposed backwardness and savagery of Haudenosaunee society. Anthropologists like Morgan often worked with the US government to create studies and academic frameworks that would facilitate military campaigns and colonial policies. Historically, once Native peoples were militarily defeated by the United States and forcibly relocated to spaces designated as reservations, which in many cases were lands undesired by white settlers, they became the places were Native people were supposed to exist and die. Like the tourists of present-day bordertowns, anthropologists would accompany Indian agents to newly formed reservations to administer government policy. Salvage ethnography became a mechanism to, on the one hand, record dying Indian cultures and, on the other, help Native people adjust to their new reality and assimilate into colonial and capitalist ideologies about labor, sex, gender, and family.

In 1953, Congress passed House Concurrent Resolution 108, which set the stage to terminate Indian tribes in California, Florida, New York, and Texas. The Klamath of Oregon and the Menominee of Wisconsin were terminated along with many smaller tribes along the West Coast. Public Law 280 allowed state governments to assume criminal and civil jurisdiction over Indian reservations in California, Minnesota, Nebraska, Oregon, and Wisconsin. In 1955, Bureau of Indian Affairs (BIA) relocation offices were established to facilitate the relocation of Native families from Native homelands into cities, where they would supposedly disappear into the multicultural milieu, thereby absolving the US government of its treaty obligations to Native nations and peoples. Hundreds of Native families were relocated to cities and towns, where they received short-term benefits, such as housing, education, and employment. They were relocated into areas where poverty and its accompanying social ills were the norm and where they were treated as second-class citizens. In 2010, the US Census reported that 78 percent of American Indians live off-reservation. Of approximately 5.2 million that self-identify as American Indian, roughly four million live off-reservation and federal trust land.

Today, many of those who reside in cities and towns are the descendants of the families relocated in the 1950s. Although often invisible in urban spaces, Native people contribute to urban and bordertown economies, while their respective nations' natural resources are exploited to benefit and create thriving urban hubs in the American West at the expense of Native land and people. In Albuquerque and places like Rapid City, South Dakota, one of the common police refrains when enacting violence on Native people is: "Go back to the reservation." Native people are seen as not belonging in bordertowns, even though these settlements are on Native land. Disturbingly, Native people today use this same logic on each other to argue that so-called urban and city Indians are inauthentic, the source of cultural death for their people.

When you subjugate a people, you not only take their land and their language, their identity, and their sense of self—you also take away any notion of a future. Native peoples' free movement across the imaginary borders of the bordertown defies binaries of rez/urban and traditional/assimilated, as do their vibrant histories of anti-colonial resistance in these spaces. Native mobility, resistance, and resilience in bordertowns pushes back against the dominant narrative that Native people are a dying, diminishing race desperately holding on to the last vestiges of their culture or their land base. If that were the case, then Standing Rock, Line 3, Bayou Bridge, the immense amount of mobilization around murdered and missing Native women, and, indeed, this book would not exist. To understand who Native people really are and not rely on government and academic jargon that seeks our disappearance, we must look at the bordertown.

Relocation

Relocation was a twentieth-century Indian removal policy. Relocation was a continuation of the 1830 Indian Removal Act, which ordered armed soldiers to forcibly march Cherokees at bayonet point from their homelands in what is currently North Carolina, west of the Mississippi River, to Indian Territory in what is currently Oklahoma. Some four thousand

Cherokees died on what became known as the "Trail of Tears." Removal first removed Natives *to* reservations, and then it proceeded to remove them *from* reservations. The first removals from reservations began when Indian agents and priests kidnapped Native children to send them to boarding schools, which aimed to "kill the Indian, save the man" through military discipline, flag worship, Christianity, and US patriotism. An untold number of Native children were murdered and generations traumatized, tortured, raped, and beaten as a result of this removal program. Removal and relocation, whether formalized in official policy or not, are always tactics of Native elimination to open the land for white settlement.

As part of the federal program of Indian termination, relocation policy set into motion the mass removal of reservation-based Natives to urban centers, such as New York, San Francisco, Denver, Minneapolis, Chicago, Cleveland, Los Angeles, and elsewhere. The goal was to eliminate Native people by removing them from the land and assimilating them into settler society. Mormon Utah senator Arthur V. Watkins adopted the language of civil rights by equating termination—in his words "the freeing of the Indian from wardship status"—to the Emancipation Proclamation, which freed slaves during the Civil War.[6] Lakota scholar Edward Valandra, however, contends that termination and relocation were little more than an attempt to overthrow Native governments, an attempt that many Native nations successfully resisted, but not unscathed.[7]

In 1953, US Congress passed House Concurrent Resolution 108 immediately terminating the federal status of the Flathead, Klamath, Menominee, Potawatomi, and Turtle Mountain Chippewa tribes. That same year, Public Law 280 authorized states to assume criminal and civil jurisdiction over Native lands. Three years later, Congress passed the Indian Relocation Act to further remove Natives from the reservation. The consequences were devastating. From 1953 to 1964, more than one hundred Native nations were terminated, and 1.3 million acres of Native land was removed from trust status to be converted into private ownership. Termination ended federal and treaty responsibilities, including access to education and health care. From the 1950s to the 1980s, as many as 750,000 Natives were relocated to cities.

Termination and relocation policy also coincided and worked in tandem with large public works projects that removed Natives from their homelands. For Missouri River Native communities, for example, the 1944 Pick-Sloan Plan authorized the Army Corps of Engineers to build five earthen-rolled dams that deliberately flooded reservation lands. As a result, 30 percent of Lakota and Dakota people living along the river were removed from their homes in the 1950s and 1960s. Because it coincided with termination and relocation, the Pick-Sloan Plan, Vine Deloria Jr. argues, "was without a doubt, the single most destructive act ever perpetrated on any tribe by the United States."[8]

As a result of removal, most Natives today do not live on reservation lands, but this does not mean they do not live on Native land. In fact, bordertowns and colonial settlements called cities have been and will always be Native land. Nevertheless, many Native people, facing dire poverty and in search of work, willfully relocate to bordertowns, where they face increased state surveillance and policing.

Savage/Savagery

The use of the word *savage*, and the claim by European settlers of Native "savagery," is more than merely a common slur used to describe Native people or a rationale for settler violence—though it surely was and remains both of these things. Use of the adjective *savage* dates to the thirteenth century and was usually a reference to something or some place that was wild, fierce, and ferocious. Its use as a noun came later and was meant to embody the condition of being "untamed," usually as a reference to any and all who would stand against establishment order.

Savage always implies movement. In Europe, the "savage" was the central problem in the collapse of feudalism. With the birth of capitalism came an unpredictable and uncontrollable mobility among a peasantry that refused capture and resisted the relations of capitalist wage labor. What came to be called the "vagabond savage" threatened the conditions necessary for capitalist accumulation. His—and it was nearly always a man—"savage" mobility refused a social order that required a constantly available laboring poor to be exploited. In the grammar of capitalism, the savage is the antonym of the obedient worker. In the grammar of nationalism, the savage is the opposite of the dutiful citizen or settler.

Henry Mayhew, the nineteenth-century English journalist, compiled an extensive study of London's poor, and like most "reformers" of his time (and ours), he saw poverty as a function of biology or a pathology of the poor. Thus, there existed in the city "two distinct and broadly marked races, viz., the wanderers and the settlers—the vagabond and the citizen—the nomadic and the civilized tribes." And this distinction was important, because, "despite the privations, its dangers, and its hardships, those who have once adopted the savage and wandering mode of life, rarely abandon it."[9]

The mobility of the "savage" is, thus, what defines the savage. Vagrancy, which is defined as the condition of one standing outside or refusing the wage relation, threatens civilization. Civilization, which is defined as the condition of class order, is, thus, the primary goal of the capitalist state. The inauguration of class order was and remains the duty and primary object of the state, usually accomplished by police. Civilization in its contemporary usage always refers to a violent police practice that describes a class order defined by compulsory citizenship, forced settlement, and wage labor.

The term *savage* today retains the reference to unacceptable mobility and the condition of one standing outside of establishment order but is used most frequently now as a slur to describe Native people—either collectively or individually. When used to describe a Native collective, it relies on a common settler typology of indigeneity—the *noble savage*.

Consider the phrase *noble savage*. The noun *savage* in *noble savage* places Native people forever outside civilization. It does this to offer a historical rationale for settler inevitability. In other words, if "civilization" (recall the definition above) is the telos of human social organization, then the settler is necessary as *the* social formation. And the adjective *noble* imagines an innate desire for civilization among those who are *savage*. This desire is unknowable to the "savage," who, according to the settler, stands forever outside history. And, even more, it is up to the settler to bring this innate desire for civilization to the surface. The job of the settler is to eradicate the worldview of the "savage" and replace it with the worldview of the settler.

Savage is, therefore, a word that names a subject who refuses but cannot be allowed to exist outside of relations and conditions of capitalist and colonial conquest. Therefore, the continued usage of the word demonstrates the abject failure of settler colonialism's primary goal—the elimination of the Native.

Church

There is a joke in Indian Country. When the Europeans came, they had the Bible and the Indians had the land. Now the Indians have the Bible and the Europeans have the land. This is the story of the New World.

In 1511, on the island that later became Cuba, the Taíno leader Hatuey orchestrated a successful resistance movement against European invaders. At the heart of the struggle was his strident opposition to the Christian church for its violent conversion of Indian souls and lands into the possessions of the Spanish Crown. "They tell us, these tyrants," he said of the Christian missionaries, "that they adore a God of peace and equality, and yet they usurp our land and make us their slaves. They speak to us of an immortal soul and of their eternal rewards and punishments, and yet they rob our belongings, seduce our women, violate our daughters." After his capture and torture in 1512, the invaders tied Hatuey to a stake to be publicly executed, a punishment befitting only the pagans of the Promised Land. Being a generous Christian, a priest offered Hatuey eternal salvation as an alternative to eternal damnation—accept Jesus Christ as his lord and savior and his soul would enter the Kingdom of Heaven. The resistance leader contemplated his situation and asked if there were Christians in heaven. The priest answered yes. Hatuey said he'd rather go to hell where there are no cruel people like the Christians. Being faithful servants, the Christians granted his request by burning him alive.

Once the church—its clergy and armies of men—became the authority of the Crown (also known as "the sovereign"), the sovereign pushed for the colonization of new lands in search of gold and souls. The Indian's body and the Indian's land, the pope and his legions argued in the Doctrine of Discovery, had to be converted into church property.

Even the name "Indian" interpellated their role in this system of organized theft and plunder. Russell Means, the late Oglala leader of the American Indian Movement, argued that, contrary to popular belief, the name "Indian" didn't come from a confused Christopher Columbus who mistakenly believed that he had landed in what was then Hindustan and what is today India. According to Means, the word *Indian* derived from Columbus's original Spanish description of the people of the Americas. Columbus called them *una gente en dio*, or simply *en dio* or *indio*: "people in god." These "peace-loving and generous" people, Columbus concluded, "would make excellent slaves." Thus, out of benevolence for these savage lands and savage people, Europeans could enslave, rape, torture, and kill them as Indians, as people in god. Means concluded that it must be as Indians that Indians fight for freedom. And once the chains of colonialism are broken: "We can call ourselves any damn thing we please!"[10]

Nature

"The idea of nature," according to Raymond Williams, "contains, though often unnoticed, an extra-ordinary amount of human history." It is through ideas of nature, according to Williams, that boundaries are erected and defended in ways that delineate human history from nonhuman history. "One touch of nature may make the whole world kin, but usually," he asks, "when we say nature, do we mean to include ourselves?"[11] Ideas of nature, in other words, are always ways to invite belonging at the same time as they are a means to enforce exclusion. In the settler colonial imagination, ideas of nature provide the central rationale and legal basis for claims to land. Indians, settlers have long argued—in a discursive construction central to all settler colonial societies—live in a *state of nature*, while the settlers' relationship to nature is one of *domination*.

The settler claims a right to dominate Native life and land. This is the sine qua non of settler colonialism. This claimed right underwrites settler violence. It is a violence posed as righteous by the settler by depicting settler domination as inherently progressive, in that it creates and defends the conditions and relations necessary for the permanent settler occupation of Native land. Some of these forms and modes of domination, based as they are on ideas of nature, appear precisely as they are: the violent expansion of white settlements on Native land through the transformation of social and natural relations. This is a version of "progress" celebrated as the taming of a "wild frontier" necessary to build a "civilization." The "frontier" in the settler imaginary is depicted as a geographical location freely available for the inevitable expansion of settler society. But "the frontier" in the settler imaginary is a people not a place. The frontier is defined as an uninhabited wilderness only through a very specific kind of settler alchemy in which Native people, living in a "state of nature," require the settler. And this is true whether we are talking about the violent dispossession of Native land by armed settlers or the romanticized notions of Native spirituality celebrated and practiced by New Age wealthy white people sweating in lodges in Sedona, Arizona.

This version of nature that the settler finds in "the frontier" poses an existential threat to the settler. Frederick Jackson Turner, the American apostle of settler domination, locates this jeopardy in the way that the frontier "masters the colonist." The settler domination of nature requires coming into contact with nature. The frontier "strips off the garments of civilization." The frontier "takes [the colonist] from the railroad car and puts him in the birch canoe. It strips off the garments of civilization and arrays him in the hunting shirt and the moccasin. It puts him in the log cabin of the Cherokee and Iroquois and runs an Indian palisade around him."[12] It is in "the frontier" that we find the first settlers playing Indian. "Before long," according to Turner, "[the colonist] has gone to planting Indian corn and plowing with a sharp stick, he shouts the war cry and takes the scalp in orthodox Indian fashion. In short, at the frontier the environment is at first too strong for the man." Nature, in other words, threatens to trap the settler in a world defined by the Native. And, so, the settler must overcome this, must first and fully understand Native life, in order to destroy it. "[The colonist]," Turner explains, "must accept the conditions which [Native life] furnishes, or perish, and so he fits himself into the Indian clearings and follows the Indian trails." And through this domination, the settler doesn't just replace the Native, the settler *becomes* the Native. In the process, something new emerges—Turner calls it "America."

Poverty

Poverty is an inevitability in liberal capitalist society, not an accident or an aberration. The only shared characteristic of those who "suffer" from "poverty" is the wage relation. The "poor" are trapped in, or excluded from, low-wage jobs in insecure industries. They are trapped, because they have only their labor to sell. Ignore those who seek after the causes of poverty—and all the many afflictions that economic insecurity produce—in the imaginary pathologies of the poor. If you're looking for the roots of poverty, start with the wage relation.

Poverty, in other words, is a relation, not a condition. It does not exist independent of the socioeconomic system that produces it. There is an impoverished class trapped in the prison of poverty. The labor of this impoverished class sustains an affluent class, for whom the labor of those who work for a living is nothing more than a "resource" for the production of more wealth. But this is more than an antagonistic relation, it is a power relation. The wage relation serves "at the same time as a means of exploitation of, and domination over, the worker."[13] If we seek the roots of the domination at the heart of the wage relation, we must start with colonial conquest.

Poverty is, therefore, a weapon, not a description. The United States federal government and various state agencies administer a variety of carefully underfunded "anti-poverty" programs. These programs—often coming in the form of welfare payments conditioned on the performance of various indignities to which the poor must submit—reinforce the relations that sustain poverty.

Poverty is indeed a settler concept, and it is deployed specifically to interrupt radical relations of solidarity. "Poverty" is a carefully calibrated counterinsurgent logic that settlers rely on to "pacify currents of rebellion," as Radmilla Cody and Brandon Benallie describe in the foreword to this volume.

Poverty is the logic underpinning anti-Indian common sense. Various federal and state programs administer anti-poverty programs, such as grants for education in white institutions, job training programs for low-wage work in white-dominated industries, or vouchers for food or other goods redeemable only in settler-owned businesses. These programs function specifically as colonial bounties. Consider the 1980 US Supreme Court decision in the *United States v. Sioux Nation of Indians*. The court found that the United States violated its own treaty when it seized and occupied He Sapa in the Black Hills, known among settlers as Mount Rushmore. The Oceti Sakowin, however, refused the $106,000,000 "award." Given that life expectancy among the Pine Ridge Lakota, for example, is nearly half that of settler society and infant mortality more than twice (statistics that settlers use to define Indian "poverty"), why would the Great Sioux Nation refuse such a windfall? Since 1980, the payout remains in a settler bank, accruing interest, now valued at nearly $1,000,000,000. But, as Roxanne Dunbar-Ortiz explains, "The Sioux believe that accepting the money would validate the US theft of their most sacred land."[14] The money cannot resolve what settlers call "poverty," because what settlers call poverty is not an Indian pathology but a colonial occupation.

And you will find all of this—the conquest and the exploitation and the cultural appropriation—in "Burn Your Village to the Ground," a track released in the United States on Thanksgiving Day 2014 by the First Nations DJ collective A Tribe Called Red. The track mocks settler explanations of Indian poverty, as it blends hip-hop and electronic Pow Wow over a sampled movie scene:

> You have taken the land which is rightfully ours
> Years from now, my people will be forced to live in mobile homes
> on reservations

Your people will wear cardigans and drink highballs
We will sell our bracelets by the roadsides
You will play golf and enjoy hot hors d'oeuvres
My people will have pain and degradation
Your people will have stick-shifts
The gods of my tribe have spoken
They have said, "Do not trust the Pilgrims"
And for all these reasons, I have decided to scalp you and burn your
village to the ground[15]

Public Education

In 2019, New Mexico ranked last out of fifty states for quality of education. Seventy-two percent of students in New Mexico public schools are low-income and over one-quarter are food-insecure. Many receive their only meal of the day through school lunch programs. New Mexico offers one of the lowest wages for public school teachers in the country and consistently posts among the lowest graduation rates in the country. Native students in New Mexico receive among the worst public educations in the United States. They graduate high school at rates between 45 percent to 65 percent, significantly lower than the already dismal statewide average. At least 60 percent of Native students who do graduate from New Mexico public schools require remediation in college, which means that two-thirds of Native students aren't prepared for postsecondary education.[16]

The landmark 2018 *Yazzie/Martinez v. State of New Mexico* court decision found that New Mexico violated its own constitutional mandate to provide adequate education to at risk students. This decision also found New Mexico in violation of the New Mexico Indian Education Act, which requires the state to provide adequate and culturally relevant education to Native students in consultation with Native nations. A few short months after the *Yazzie/Martinez* decision by the First Judicial District Court in Santa Fe, a white Albuquerque high school teacher committed what then Navajo Nation president Russell Begaye called "cultural assault" against two Native students by forcibly cutting one student's hair after asking the student if she "liked her braids" and calling another a "bloody Indian" for donning fake blood on her face as part of her Halloween costume.[17] The incident made national news and fanned the flames of growing Native outrage at the anti-Indianism at the heart of state's public education program.

Add to this the fact that New Mexico depends on revenues from resource extraction on tribal lands to fund postsecondary education, a practice that pollutes Native land and violates the consent of many Native communities, and you get a clear picture of "public education": a state institution that is anti-Indian through and through. While exceptionally incompetent and negligent, the State of New Mexico isn't unique. Its spectacular anti-Indianism illustrates the rule of bordertown violence: where Native people and nations abound in numbers that defy the colonial designs of elimination, anti-Indian discrimination and violence proliferate to keep Native presence in check.

Quality education is tied to all other forms of social and economic well-being. If Native people escape the violence of police and vigilantes, they still need to contend with racist policy makers and educators. This leaves Native people in a position of permanent disadvantage when it comes to jobs, health, housing, and other socioeconomic indicators. It is because of this track record in education that Red Power activists fought for Native American Studies departments in American universities in the 1960s, as well as survival schools to replace K–12 education, as a means to rectify the extreme anti-Indianism that Native children confront in mainstream public education.

CHAPTER THREE

Indian Killers

Indian Rolling

Scholars, lawyers, and journalists have framed Indian rolling as a type of extreme hate crime against Native people. Indian rolling is extreme because of the exceptionally brutal methods of torture that its perpetrators use to harm and murder Native people, including beating, bludgeoning (rocks and cinder blocks are common), burning, and mutilating (especially genitalia). Indian rollers typically target unsheltered Native people, elders, and those compromised by intoxication.

The term *Indian rolling* first appeared in 1974 during protests in the wake of the Chokecherry Massacre in Farmington, New Mexico. One of the protest organizers, John Redhouse, explained Indian rolling as a kind of blood sport:

> We didn't see the murders as the act of three crazy kids. We saw it as a part of a whole racist picture. For years it has been almost a sport, a sort of sick, perverted tradition among Anglo youth of Farmington High School, to go into the Indian section of town and physically assault and rob elderly and sometimes intoxicated Navajo men and women of whatever possession they had, for no apparent reason, other than that they were Indians.[1]

Redhouse notes that, like any hate crime, Indian rolling is driven by racism against Native—in the case of Farmington, Navajo—people. However, framing Indian rolling as a hate crime limits our understanding of how Indian rolling as a type of settler violence is part of the larger structure of settler colonialism. Reducing Indian rolling to a hate crime obscures the fact that Indian killing serves a structural purpose in a settler society premised on the elimination of Native peoples. Indian rolling is simply the enforcement of the settler order of things by settlers who are carrying out this larger project of Native elimination. Indian rolling is often gendered, with Hispano and white settler boys and men carrying out the majority of Indian killings in bordertowns. But the blood sport of Indian rolling isn't carried out by vigilantes and settler citizens alone. It is also carried out every time a cop bludgeons, beats, maims, or tortures a Native person in the name of settler law and order.

Indian rolling is a type of lynching; the settler order literally carved and burned into the bodies of Native people. Although it enforces and reinforces the elimination of Native people, Indian rolling also serves a pedagogical and social regulation function in off-reservation spaces; it conveys the message that Native people don't belong "off the reservation" and are not welcome in settler towns and cities where they are expected to have been cleared and disappeared by previous colonial campaigns. Because there are high numbers of Native people in bordertowns, their presence upsets settler expectations for Native erasure and subjugation. Therefore, settler vigilantes and cops work to terrorize Native people; to remind them that they are forever "out of place" in a settler world. The terrorism of Indian rolling is not extreme or unusual; it is engrained in the social fabric of settler identity and kinship in the United States, particularly among men in bordertowns, home of the Indian killers.

Vigilante

A vigilante is commonly defined as a private citizen who takes the law into their own hands to avenge what they perceive as a crime or to defend against what is perceived as a threat. A vigilante makes or upholds the law in the perceived absence of it. On the frontier, vigilantism flourishes as an essential practice of settler colonialism, by upholding civilization and claiming its own nonexistence in Indian Country. From what and from whom must civilization be defended?

The German philosopher Georg Hegel once credited European liberal democracies with inventing "civil society" or "bourgeois society." Invoking civil society or "civility" also invokes an antagonistic, although often unacknowledged, opposite: "savage society" or "savagery"—in other words, the darker nations and territories Europeans intend to "civilize" and bring order to. When Frederick Jackson Turner celebrated US imperial expansion in his "frontier thesis," he defined "the outer edge of the wave" of invasion as "the meeting point between savagery and civilization."[2] The latter would replace the former. At this meeting point, known as the frontier, Indian Country was seen as a lawless landscape, and the Indian was made into a lawless criminal, a "merciless Indian savage" who threatened US empire. But the frontier has not closed, nor is it confined to a specific time or place. Instead, the frontier is a practice of policing space and people, created and recreated wherever the Indian persists.

A settler's hypervigilance against the Indian's persistence makes him a vigilante, authorized to carry out the law, with genocidal violence if necessary. Put another way, settler vigilantism is *law outside of law*, and, thus, makes the law. Law is not a civilizing force or an objective standard, it is a means to shore up the legitimacy of those who use violence to fabricate and defend order. The vigilante exists for this purpose, because, as every settler knows, *settler society must be defended!* Indian persistence is a constant reminder of the settler's own tenuous belonging. The settler as vigilante is, thus, the bearer of a murderous civilizational order. Throughout history the vigilante came as conquistador, explorer, frontiersman, trapper, poacher, slave catcher, trader, cowboy, militiaman, cop, oilman, pipeline worker, and armed citizen.

The cowboy, portrayed as a heroic gunslinger in popular culture, idealizes the settler vigilante. In western films, such as John Ford's 1956 classic *The Searchers*, for example, settler vigilantism is depicted as a form of self-defense. In this version, it is the settler not the Indian who is surrounded. John Wayne, the archetypical cowboy, plays an ex-Confederate soldier killing his way through Comanche territory. On the post–Civil War frontier, North and South united in Indian killing. Native genocide in *The Searchers* is shown as an act of revenge for killing a white squatter and taking his daughter. The crime, in this case, is not invasion but Native self-defense. The "cowboy as Indian killer" also upholds the myth of rugged individualism, a fetishized settler identity forged and constantly remade through violence. But invaders never come as individuals, otherwise they easily would have been dispatched. Indian killers come armed with the support of the colonial state and are mobilized by the collective will of settler society, raping, murdering, beating, torturing, and plundering their way to civilization.

Ending vigilante violence against Native people was a primary cause the Red Power Movement took as its own. On a cold winter night in February 1972, in Gordon, Nebraska, a bordertown to the Pine Ridge Indian Reservation, four white men—Melvin and Leslie Hare, Bernard Ludder, and Robert Bayless—kidnapped fifty-one-year-old Oglala elder Raymond Yellow Thunder. The men stripped Yellow Thunder naked, beat him, forced him to dance as a "drunk Indian" for the entertainment of whites in a dance hall, before leaving him to die from his wounds. Outraged, Yellow Thunder's family called on the American Indian Movement, who quickly mobilized and took Gordon by storm. Without pressure from AIM, Leslie and Marvin Hare would have walked. To memorialize Yellow Thunder and all those Native people ruthlessly abused and murdered by settler vigilantes, the "Raymond Yellow Thunder Song" became the "AIM Song." Vigilantism is an organizing principle of settler colonialism.

Police Violence

Police violence rarely comes into focus. Something close to it comes into view when we use the phrase *police brutality*, but that phrase implies that the police use of force (a euphemism for police violence) is something other than violence. Police violence is often understood as having a dual character—it can either be unjustified, which often gets called "police brutality," or it can be justified, which gets called "the police use of force." When police violence is misunderstood as having this dual nature, activists' calls to end "police brutality" function as calls to expand police violence—give us less police brutality and more justified police use of force.

To bring police violence into focus, we should start by recognizing that police are violence specialists. The job of policing is to fabricate social order and to rely on violence or the threat of violence to make this order. What exactly is the order that police fabricate? This is an important question. When we engage in an analysis of police that does not begin with this question, we leave it up to police to provide an explanation for their violence. And when this happens, police are only too happy to explain away their violence as something other than violence. It is force, and it is necessary to "serve and protect," cops tell us. But policing in settler societies like the United States, Canada, Australia, New Zealand, and Israel has always been the work of fabricating a settler social order. All settler colonial policing begins with the idea that Native peoples have no claim to Native land and, equally important, stand in the way of settler claims to Native land. The order that police create is a settler order that requires the elimination of the Native conditioned by a settler claim over Native land

and Native life and a settler obligation to bring about Native death. While the obligation to manage Native life and death is distributed broadly among settler citizens, it is the very job of police. Police are Indian killers.

To speak of bordertown violence is to speak of the vigilante who beats up a Native man in a bordertown or the cop who kills a Native woman on the street or the payday lender who traps a Native family in a ruthless cycle of debt. To speak of police violence, however, is to speak very specifically of what Mark Neocleous calls the "permissive structure of law." Law accommodates police. Police are always "beyond the law," yet their behavior is also always "lawful." And since law is about order not justice, what might seem trivial on its surface, such as the mere presence of a Native person in a bordertown, is seen to police as among the gravest of threats to good order. The Indian killer, therefore, is law itself.

Don't look to law to rescue us from police violence. Law explicitly endorses violence against Native peoples. And don't call for an end to police brutality, which is nothing more than a call for more and better police trained to inflict more humane and efficient violence and, thus, more "good order" in the bordertown. Instead, call for an end to police violence, which is a call for the end of police and, thus, the end of settler social order.

Indian Expert

"Indians have been cursed above all other people," wrote Standing Rock Sioux scholar Vine Deloria Jr. "They have anthropologists."[3] And pawn-brokers. And Christian missionaries. And traders. And Indian agents. And bureaucrats. And other parasites who infest Indian Country. In the early nineteenth century, Indian experts murdered men, women, and children for scalp contracts. In the late nineteenth century, Indian experts claimed to have been kidnapped by Indians and wrote breathless memoirs of captivity and escape. In the early twentieth century, Indian experts worked at Bureau of Indian Affairs hospitals sterilizing women and girls. In the late twentieth century, Indian experts became "scholars" of "public health" and epidemiology and wrote books about "drunk Indians." The Indian Expert always "tells it like it is," as Deloria puts it, which is to say that the job of the Indian Expert has always been to keep attention on various Indian pathologies and away from the organizing violence of the settler society. The job of the Indian Expert is to depict the vanishing Indian, the corrupted Indian, the Indian as a shadow of what the Indian once was.

Dark humor and dramatic irony percolate through Deloria's often hilarious satire of anthropology, but make no mistake, he is deadly serious. "The fundamental thesis of the anthropologist is that people are objects for observation, people are then considered objects for experimentation, for manipulation, and for eventual extinction."[4] There is no more important job among settlers in a settler society than the job of the Indian Expert. The role of the Indian Expert, and the various modes it takes, can be summarized by its four essential colonial tasks.

The first task of the Indian Expert is to represent Indians as responsible for the genocidal violence of settler colonialism. These "experts," who once issued scalp bounties and wrote travelogues and captivity narratives, now cash checks from prestigious Ivy League institutions for their "field research."

The second task of the Indian Expert is to provide the legal, biological, economic, and cultural rationale for genocidal policies that include child abduction (also known as boarding school), sterilization, Indian removal, treaty violations, and too many others to mention. They design "studies" of Indian pathology and publish articles in "scientific" journals about Indian biology and genetics, in which they claim Indians are unfit for modern life. They give interviews to fawning reporters in offices decorated by looted headdresses and tomahawks incoherently displayed.

The third task of the Indian Expert is to place Indians forever in the past. Indians have vanished these "experts" explain, but at least we have all their stuff. This is how the Indian Expert as a class transforms Indians into a settler economy. The Indian Expert takes a life and transforms it into an artifact and the artifact into a commodity and the commodity into an economy.

The last task of the Indian Expert, a task only recently added, is to modernize the role of the Indian Expert in settler society. To survive, settler colonialism must appear as what it is not. So Indian experts hold degrees in "Indian" law and draft administrative law regulations for BIA bureaucracies to "help" Native people, which is another way to take children from their homes. They hold elected office and pass payday loan legislation for bordertown "economic development," which is another way to loot Indian art and artists. They own and control hospitals that continue to offer reproductive health services, which is another way to sterilize women and girls. They "play Indian" in cities like Sedona or Flagstaff or Rapid City or Santa Fe, where they claim to have tapped into some profound Native spirituality, which is another way to depict "The Indian" as a product of settler society.

The Indian Expert works to resolve the fundamental contradiction of settler colonialism, which is that its future is conditioned on settler society's capacity to sustain genocide. While the job of the Indian Expert has always been to manage this insecurity, the contemporary Indian Expert operates differently. The Indian Expert today pretends to be a real ally with Native peoples by claiming "cultural competency." These Indian experts demonstrate their "cultural competency" when they place Indians as one among many deserving "identities" that inhabit the settler's liberal multicultural society. The point here is to stifle Indigenous solidarity, to thwart the possibility of international solidarity among Native peoples, and to undermine solidarity among Native peoples, Black and Chicanx folks, immigrants, the poor, and the working class.

The Indian Expert does not wear a target on its back. We must place it there.

Drunk Tank

Four decades ago, Gallup, New Mexico, was so notorious for its public display of drunkenness that the city became known as "Drunk Town, USA." The ABC television program 20/20 solidified Gallup's reputation as "Drunk Town, USA" with a 1987 segment about Gallup that included photographs of bodies piled into what was known colloquially as the city's "drunk tank." These were the bodies of Navajo men who had been picked up by police and then taken into "protective custody." Protective custody meant that police arrested anyone they claimed was inebriated in public spaces. They held hundreds of people in a 4,800-square-foot drunk tank cell with a cement floor, a drain, and nothing more. Police routinely filled the jail so beyond capacity that people slept on the floor in shifts, taking turns standing for hours awaiting their turn to lie on the hard concrete.

As a 1950s survey of Navajos and Hopis in Gallup reported, the police viewed public drunkenness as the largest problem they confronted, which was largely attributed to Navajos coming off the Navajo reservation to buy and consume liquor. In the 1970s, Gallup ranked nationally as first in alcohol-related deaths, with Gallup's McKinley County the worst county in the United States for alcohol-related mortality. Residents there were 225 percent more likely to die from alcohol-related causes than were New Mexico residents overall. In 1973, New Mexico decriminalized public drunkenness and created a category it called "protective custody." Under the law, individuals deemed inebriated could be held for twelve hours. By the 1980s, police claimed that they spent most of their time picking up inebriated people and depositing them in the drunk tank. Today, the National Institute of Alcohol Abuse and Alcoholism estimates that the area surrounding McKinley County has the worst alcoholism problem in the nation, though it doesn't provide a precise definition of "alcoholism." On average, twenty-six thousand people are taken into protective custody each year in Gallup for alcohol-related incidents, and the area's rate of alcohol-related traffic accidents is twice the state average.

In response to protests and ongoing negative media attention, Gallup implemented a number of measures, including closing nearly a half-dozen Gallup bars and banning Sunday liquor sales and walk-up windows at liquor stores. McKinley County approved a liquor excise tax, which generated nearly $600,000 annually for abuse prevention and educa-tion. Further, Gallup's Driving While Intoxicated (DWI) ordinance (a 0.08 blood alcohol level or greater leading to seventy-two hours of mandatory jail time for first-time offenders) is the strictest in the state. Longtime New Mexico Republican senator Pete Domenici also supported Gallup's efforts by advocating for the federal government to allocate $900,000 through Indian Health Service to operate a new protective custody center, which became Na'Nizhoozhi Center (NCI). Using city and federal funds, NCI opened its doors in 1992, thereby closing the doors of the notorious city drunk tank profiled five years earlier by 20/20. Between 1992 and 2012, NCI served as a detox center, a short-term shelter, a provider of treatment for DWI offenders, and a counseling unit. NCI also initiated a fourteen-day program utilizing traditional Native healing methods to help chronic alcoholics. In the 1980s, Gallup averaged a little more than 34,000 protective-custody admissions to the drunk tank each year. By 1996, admissions to NCI had dropped to 17,723.

While NCI's methods saw some success, its existence was short-lived, and Gallup continues to criminalize Native people for drinking. In the years following its opening, NCI was criticized by those who experienced its services. The Gallup Police Department created a new subdivision of policing called Community Service Aides to patrol and sweep Gallup's streets for intoxicated individuals who were then transported to NCI. Data gathered by the Navajo Nation Human Rights Commission indicates that these transports are often involuntary, and that patrol surveillance leads Native people to hide or elude service aides to avoid detention at NCI. Many claimed it was no different than the city's drunk tank of earlier years. Stories about walking down Gallup streets (inebriated or not) only to be targeted and detained by Community Service officers were common. Many told stories of being forced to take a breath analyzer test, only to find themselves thrown into the NCI "drunk tank."

For a brief period, the Navajo Nation took over the operation of NCI, and, by 2012, Gallup expressed concerns that NCI faced closure. In 2017, NCI received funding to keep its doors open and to offer treatment services for substance use and provide shelter. The congressional appropriation will be made annually until 2022. After more than fifty years of attention to Gallup's "problem," not much has changed in its landscape of public intoxication and its accompanying social ills and atmosphere of racism and discrimination against its Native population. McKinley County is the poorest county in New Mexico, and its largest city, Gallup, has the highest concentration of predatory lending stores that target poor Navajos on- and off-reservation. The city is home to a multimillion-dollar-a-year liquor industry, with thirty-nine liquor licenses (more per capita than most major cities) that exploit already vulnerable Native people. Native, mostly Navajo, dollars keep the Gallup economy afloat, yet Natives have no political power in the city. Navajos and other Natives continue to meet unnatural and largely uninvestigated or under-investigated deaths in Gallup connected to the toxic environment of alcohol saturation. Drunk tanks, as a feature of bordertowns like Gallup, are but one signifier of how settler colonialism plays out in the present.

Forced Sterilization

In January 1973, Victor Cutnose, along with five other men, seized control of the Gallup Indian Medical Center. Armed with rifles and explosives, the men demanded the dismissal of hospital staff, including doctors, they deemed "disrespectful" to Native peoples. The Gallup Indian Medical Center was notorious for its treatment of Native men, women, and children. It was there and at the surrounding boarding schools that Indian Health Service (IHS) doctors conducted human trials on Navajo children and performed forced sterilizations of Native women as part of what doctors considered routine practice.

The armed occupation of the Gallup hospital occurred during the height of IHS policies to forcibly sterilize Native women. There are hundreds, if not thousands, of studies on the forced sterilization of Native people in the United States, and nearly all conclude that IHS sterilized between 25 and 50 percent of all Native American women between the years 1970 and 1976. IHS doctors continued to sterilize Native women even after a 1973 US District Court moratorium was placed on sterilization. A 1976 US Congressional investigation of four IHS service areas in the US Southwest, which included Gallup and Albuquerque, concluded that the IHS sterilized 3,406 Native women between 1973 and 1976.

Sterilization is not an official state practice imposed only on Native women. It has been a common eugenicist practice imposed via official state institutions on incarcerated, Black, Hispanic, and poor white women throughout the twentieth century. Eugenics is the racist idea that some people have no right or a limited right to reproduction, because members of these racial groups, according to eugenecists, are genetically less intelligent and, therefore, beyond the reach of social progress. The state, according to this logic, is obligated to manage the distribution of reproductive rights only to those deemed "fit," which has historically meant the white (and settler) body politic. Eugenics is the pseudoscience of white supremacy, and it structures the work of establishment scientific institutions throughout the United States.

But the forced sterilization of Native women cannot be explained solely though the logic of eugenics. All settler states are sterilizing states. This is to say that all settler states employ eugenics as a tactic of genocide. The forced sterilization of Native women and, to a lesser degree, men is part of the genocidal logic of Native elimination. Sterilization, like the theft of children from Native households, is one way that settler states control the perceived threat that Native overpopulation presents to settler demographic supremacy. Settlers try to prevent the so-called Indian hordes from rising again to burn down their forts. They worry constantly that Native peoples will outnumber them and overthrow the settler logic of "kill to replace," which must remain intact for settler order to maintain its dominance on stolen land. The forced sterilization of Native women, like settler colonialism, is, at the end of the day, about land. The only response is decolonization.

Gender Violence

Gender violence includes sexual violence, genital mutilation, child marriage, sex trafficking, domestic violence, abduction of girls, bride kidnappings, war brides, sexual harassment at the workplace, emotional or physical violence, femicide, coercive reproductive practices, and rape. Most normative understandings of gender violence rely on a binary of men/women and masculine/feminine in order to define violence as a product of social inequalities between men and women. When invoked this way, gender binaries serve as both an explanation and a basis for inequalities that place women at a lower social and economic status than men and do not speak to how settler colonialism structures gender.

Gender as a binary disguises the role of gender violence in constituting settler colonialism. According to Deborah Miranda, Native peoples practiced gender diversity prior to European, and then American, settler invasions. Such diversity incurred the wrath of Spanish priests in colonial Spanish California, where Jesuit priests systematically and ruthlessly tortured Native peoples. They focused their violence on those they believed to be *joyas*, "queer," or a third gender, and they sought to exterminate the third genders they encountered in Native societies.[5] Gender violence, therefore, is a foundational settler colonial practice. Settlers declare as abnormal anything that diverts from the binary man/woman. To be queer is to be criminal to the settler, and so the settler state seeks to exterminate and erase the presence of genders beyond the masculine/feminine binary.

As Native and queer feminists point out, the "queer" represents a political and social order threatening to the settler nation and its citizens. We value the presence of our nonbinary relatives. We know their importance in our survival as a people. We remember the stories our ancestors told us about our third-, fourth-, and fifth-gendered relatives within our kin networks—in Diné as *nádleehí* and in Lakota as *winkte*—and value these relatives as gifted persons. In solidarity movements that refuse settler values, including patriarchy, the nuclear family, and property ownership, we invoke our original teachings about kinship extended to all human beings and to all other than human beings. Confronting gender violence through queer-affirming networks liberates us from the pathology of heteronormative settler thinking. The world isn't heteronormative, only the settler world is. There is no end to gender violence in a settler world. If we seek to build and nurture a community that extends relations to all beings, the Earth and Sky, and other than human relatives, we would do well to remember the stories our ancestors told us and look to the gifted persons to help us.[6]

MMIWG2S: Missing and Murdered Native Women, Girls, and Two-Spirit People

Anthonette Cayedito. Fred C. Martinez. Rose Osborne. Cecelia Finona. Raymond Yellow Thunder. Chris Yazzie. Betty Osbourne. Anna Mae Aquash. Brandy Wesaquate. Allison Gorman. Ella Johnson. Pamela George. Kee Thompson. Ashley Utley. Sherry Quintero-Davenport. Belinda Williams. Tanya Holyk. Laney Ewenin. Loreal Tsingine. Patricia Felinian Miranda. Irma Arce Garcete. Rose Osborne. Nee Oliver Yazzie. Ronnie Ross. Amy Hansen. Loretta Saunders. Hannah Harris.

These are the names of Native women, girls, transwomen, and Two-Spirits who have been murdered or gone missing. Some of the names may be familiar, but most are not. It has been through the dogged work of families, Native women's groups, and community-based organizations that we know anything at all about the people listed here. And it is because of the persistence of families and relatives that some of the victims have seen some measure of justice through the settler colonial systems. This is no small feat since settler justice does not recognize that Native lives matter.

On April 6, 1986, nine-year-old Anthonette Cayedito answered a knock at the door of her family's home in Gallup, New Mexico, and was never seen again.

No one has seen fifty-nine-year old Cecelia Finona since May 30, 2020, when her family last saw her in Farmington, New Mexico. No one knows who murdered Helen Betty in 1971 in Winnipeg, Manitoba, Canada. Her sister, Rose Osborne, devoted her life to stopping the violence against women. She created the Helen Betty Memorial Foundation and worked for justice for her sister until someone murdered Rose, a Native transwoman, in 2008.

Thomas Mayes was convicted of the 1992 fatal shooting of his partner, Ella Johnson. Mayes, a Gallup cop, shot and killed Johnson in a parked car at a Gallup hotel while her twelve-year-old son watched from the back seat. He served eight years in jail. In 2005, the Santa Fe Boys and Girls Club hired him despite the conviction, because he was, "in general, a nice guy."[7]

Shaun Murphy killed Fred Martinez, a self-identified nádleehí and Two-Spirit, in 2008. A search party found her mutilated body in a remote area outside of Cortez, Colorado. Murphy bragged to friends that he beat up and killed a "fag."

The movement to get justice for the murders of Native women, girls, transwomen, and Two-Spirits is often represented by the acronym MMIWG2S, but no acronym captures the astonishing scope and scale of the violence. Thousands and thousands of women and girls go missing, but few are ever reported. Native women are more likely to be murdered than the national average, but even this statistic undercounts the violence.[8] The numbers often exclude violence against transwomen, and efforts to confront this problem that rely on statistical data or "crime" data often undercount the problem and render invisible all those who do not count as "female."[9]

LGBTQI2S people experience colonial violence and oppression in far greater numbers in relation to Native women and girls' experiences. Further, gender violence is compounded for Native people in urban spaces and bordertowns, where at least 70 percent of the population live, as a result of losses of kinship connections beyond the normative nuclear family unit and to communities on designated Native lands. Further, the movement across imaginary boundaries of Native nations and urban spaces foments dislocations, whereby women and LGBTQI2S find themselves in settler spaces devoid of kinship-based resources. Vigilantes and police prey on these relatives. Many are forced by violence or circumstances into sex work.

This profound settler gender violence defines settler social relations, particularly those with the state and its institutions, such as police, jails, courts, welfare agencies, and schools. These are institutions organized around Native disposability and make no effort to confront the problem of Native gender violence. Settler state violence shapes the response of Native nations, nearly all of which have been transformed by settler state violence and, thus, like the settler state also fail to confront gender violence.

All settler nations, founded as they are on a genocidal violence that make and sustain claims to sovereignty over Native peoples and Native land, domesticate Native nations and their people. This is accomplished by law, police and vigilante violence, and more. And this drive for Native domestication fuels the epidemic of violence against Native women, girls, and Two-Spirit people. If the settler state recognizes MMIWG2S at all, it is not to end it but, rather, to reproduce and reinforce the relations that make all of it possible. MMIWG2S will never be resolved by the settler state, for to do so requires the dismantling of settler nations.

Militarization

Militarization is a particular mode of social organization marked by legal, material, and symbolic expressions of militarism that pervade every aspect of daily life. These expressions are broadly understood as compulsory in liberal capitalist states, where ubiquitous and obligatory displays of patriotism underwrite citizenship, and where martial values (authoritarianism, conformity, social conservatism, violence, and hetero-patriarchy, among others) provide a shared, rarely contested political language and logic.

It is not enough to say that settler societies are militarized societies. While true, the claim implies that settler societies merely adopt milita-rization as a political technique or develop militarized modes of social organization to resolve the contradictions of settler colonial violence. Such a view is only partly true. While attuned to the malevolent influence of settler colonial militarization on the lives and futures of Native peoples, this developmentalist view of settler militarization fails to capture the reciprocal and etiological nature of the relationship between settler colo-nialism and militarization.

At the heart of all settler colonial societies we find an apparent and seemingly unresolvable contradiction. On the one hand, settler colonial-ism valorizes progress, individual liberty (through property), democracy, and the universal promise of safety, security, and prosperity generated by all of these. On the other hand, we find pervasive, sustained, and targeted violence organized and deployed by the settler state against Native peoples. This apparent contradiction—the realization of safety and security for settlers because of sustained, state violence against Native peoples—is not so much a contradiction, however, but, rather, should be understood as the wellspring of settler society itself.

As Audra Simpson explains, "Colonialism survives in a settler form. In this form, it fails at what it is supposed to do: eliminate Native people; take all their land; absorb them into a white, property-owning body politic."[10] Given its abject failure to eliminate Native peoples, we should ask what then sustains the settler form? When we ask this question, we find an answer in militarization. If settler safety and security exist at all, they exist as conditions of police, militia, and vigilante violence and the broad acceptance of this violence (usually rendered as lawful or justified or, if impossible to defend, ignored as aberrant or anomalous). These pat-terns are invisible to settlers and, as such, literally do not exist for settlers.

But we know there is no settler prosperity without settler law's coercive political economies of resource extraction on Native land. We know there is no settler security without police, militia, and vigilante violence against Native peoples. We know there is no settler future without the destruction of Native claims to land. And we also know, despite all of this, that the thing that sustains settler society—militarization—will also destroy it.

White Supremacy

White supremacy refers to the imagined biological and social superiority of white people, which, to white supremacists, provides the basis for claims to the social, political, and economic domination of society by white people. The scale and scope of such a claim is often described through the language of disparity. In the United States, for example, a Native woman is paid fifty-seven cents for every dollar a white man makes. US judges and juries sentence Natives to prison at over four times the rate of white people. Native people comprise 4 percent of the population of Canada, but 36 percent of all women and 25 percent of all men in Canada's jails are Native.

The language of "disparities"—whether in sentencing, educational attainment, or income—appears to merely describe the scope and scale of white supremacy. What's most important here is the way it depicts white supremacy as an aberration—as a problem of institutional racism that disproportionately impacts Native peoples. To depict white supremacy as an aberration is to presuppose an imagined and possible alternative world of perfect equality and equity, where something called white supremacy can be overcome, and where Native women will make as much money as white men, and Native people will be incarcerated at rates no different than other groups. Beware: there is no such alternative in a world full of settlers.

The language of disparities depicts the logic of elimination at the heart of settler colonialism as a kind of historical or political accident or aberration that should be confronted not through decolonization struggles over land but, rather, through political reforms to existing systems and institutions. The "white supremacy as aberration" logic seeks to blunt Native resistance to the settler state. Liberalism, in other words, is offered as the solution to white supremacy. Among the solutions liberalism offers are assimilation and state recognition, which is to say that the solution to white supremacy is found in the expansion of the settler state, which is based on and can't exist beyond white supremacy.

White supremacy, however, is better understood as an organizing logic of settler and slave society—a logic that gives meaning and momentum to settler colonial violence. White supremacy is not an aberration of the liberal capitalist state; it is its mirror image. After all, settler colonialism destroys to replace. The "disparities" that appear to describe white supremacy are not aberrations at all but, rather, reflect settler colonialism's unfinished and ongoing goal of the total dissolution of Native society. The "solutions" the liberal capitalist state offers to white supremacy are the smallpox-infected blankets of ongoing settler colonialism.

Exposure

Exposure is a leading cause of death for Native people in bordertowns, particularly unsheltered relatives. Exposure deaths increase during the winter months when low temperatures cause hypothermia and many who live and sleep outdoors freeze to death. Exposure deaths refer to unnatural deaths, or deaths that occur as a result of external forces. Unnatural deaths are the opposite of natural deaths, or deaths that occur as a result of "natural causes." While elements like heat, cold, snow, fire, and rain are common external causes of exposure deaths, exposure also refers to the increased risk that comes with being unsheltered. These risks include assault, murder, rape, theft, stalking, and arrest. Being unsheltered decreases your safety and increases the likelihood you will experience violence and harm. To be without shelter leaves you quite literally exposed and vulnerable. Therefore, we cannot address exposure without also addressing the links between the logic of homelessness and settler colonialism.

As discussed in some detail in chapter one, in July 2014, three teenagers brutally bludgeoned to death two Diné men, Allison Gorman and Kee Thompson, who were sleeping in a vacant lot on Albuquerque's Westside at the time of the attack. Jerome Eskeets, a fellow traveler and relative of Gorman, whom he called "uncle," was resting in the vacant lot when the teenagers approached. Eskeets witnessed the murders and narrowly escaped with his life. National media picked up the story immediately. During an interview with an AP journalist, Eskeets recalled the teenagers deriding the Navajo men for being "homeless" several times as they were beating them to death. As he recounted the murders, he told the reporter, "We're not homeless. Our home is right here on this land."[11]

As we note in the next section on homelessness, Native people are treated as terrorists, the original threat to US "homeland security." Settlers understand the Native act of claiming a home on the land as a threat to order. This is an existential threat to a settler society based on a claim to "virgin land," already cleared of any Native presence through waves of genocidal campaigns of removal. To proclaim that Native people living and sleeping outside are homeless is to claim they don't belong, that they constitute a foreign threat to America's security, and that the job of settler colonialism is only finished when they are cleared finally from the land.

What does this have to do with exposure? Why does sleeping and living outside—something humans have done for millennia—place Native people at risk of dying from unnatural causes? Because the condition of being unsheltered in settler society is a condition that marks one as an enemy of settler society. Vigilantes murdered Gorman and Thompson, which is how exposure works in bordertowns. In their case and those of countless other Native people in bordertowns, the condition of being unsheltered is among the conditions necessary for settler violence. It increases Native exposure to settler violence; it increases Native exposure to the Indian killers who patrol the streets of bordertowns at night; it increases Native exposure to the vigilantes who kill Indians for blood sport.

Like all people, Native people deserve shelter, and there are many reasons, including social and family violence, domestic abuse, homophobia and transphobia, poor health care, mental health issues, and housing injustice, that explain why Native people live on the streets at such high rates. These exposure deaths are one and the same with the bordertown hunts, with the constant arrests, and with the missing and murdered Native peoples that structure the settler world.

Homelessness

What counts as home? What counts as a home? Who gets to claim the lands of the United States as a homeland?

Native peoples often invoke the concept of *homelands* to describe their relationship with ancestral territories and lands. Sometimes the political boundaries of present-day Native nations match the *homelands* Native people have in mind when we use this term. More often, though, our homelands cover vast expanses that far exceed current reservation boundaries. Reservations are not homelands, they are a product of settler violence, the extreme reduction of Native homelands. Our homelands have been stolen by settler governments like the United States and carved into private property for settler landowners. The United States claims these stolen lands for itself when it declares sovereignty over "homeland security." Native homelands don't belong to the United States because the United States pilfered what it calls its homeland from Native nations. But Native nations have neither disappeared nor relinquished their rightful relationship with their homelands.

Consider the colloquial phrase "home is where the heart is." What are matters of the heart? Family. Shelter. Warmth. Love. Safety. To be homeless *and* Native means that one has no homeland, has no family, has no love, and has no safety or security. To be homeless *and* Native places one beyond care and concern, condemned to live a life without relatives, without belonging, with nothing and from nowhere. As Dakota scholar Elizabeth Cook-Lynn argues, to be outside of Native bonds of kinship and severed from our homelands is to be alien and without a future. But Native people are only alienated from settler society. We are not homeless in our own homelands. Settler common sense requires we believe that we are homeless, and settler order is the enforcement of that exclusion. To believe this is to submit to settler authority, to participate in our own destruction. To believe this is to think and act like a settler. That world erases us from the land permanently and reduces us from nations to citizens in liberal, capitalist, multicultural America. That world claims dominion "from sea to shining sea" once and for all. We have no place in that world.

We fight back against this, because the stakes are life and death. The term *homeless* first emerged in the early colonial period in North America. It referred to European settlers in New England who fled their farms in the wake of King Philip's War of 1675–1676, an uprising led by the famous Pokanoket leader Metacom. Settlers fled to coastal towns where they quickly became a new class: "vagrants." These struggles occurred alongside transformative shifts in New World mercantile capitalism, which created new categories of human surplus, for example, slaves.

As neither slaves nor settlers, however, Native people did not fall into either of these categories. Instead, they were, from the get-go, cast as insurgents and enemies of the state—terrorists. This means Native people existed outside of the subject position of the "vagrant" and, therefore, were also not subject to the logic of homelessness.

Today, we watch as cops, journalists, churches, politicians, and activists refer to unsheltered Native people as homeless, transients, or vagrants. The term *transient* is commonly found in police reports when referring to unsheltered Native people or Native people that cops simply encounter on the street. These cops aren't confused. These words aren't beside the fact. They operate within the logic of settler colonialism that dictates Native people are enemies of the state who must be annihilated—literally cleared out of the way—for US expansion to succeed. This clearing can and has happened through multiple techniques: military and police deployment, boarding schools, starvation, the kidnapping of Native children, sterilization of Native women, etc. Categorizing Native people as homeless today is a form of counterinsurgency. If we are enemies of the state—terrorists—imagine the ends to which the United States will go to suppress us with the limitless power it grants itself by the settler logic of "homeland security." It will target, detain, torture, and kill us. The settler does this with impunity, but, more importantly, the settler does it because it is compulsory. This is what "homelands" means to a settler nation like the United States. Indians won't stand aside and let settlers steal their land and future, turn them into terrorists, and beat them back until the job is done! This is America. And America will turn anyone in the world who defies US supremacy into an Indian (Osama Bin Laden as "Geronimo") and this will justify everything.

Pandemic

Tuberculosis, the great destroyer of Indian nations. Smallpox, measles, influenza, the shock troops of colonial conquest, each made a murderous march through Indian Country. Now comes SARS-CoV-2, the virus that causes Coronavirus disease 2019 (COVID-19), another severe acute respiratory syndrome attacking Native peoples. It was first identified in December 2019 in Wuhan, the capital city of Hubei province, China. Like settlers, it lurked for years before emerging on its global campaign. By January 30, 2020, the World Health Organization declared the virus an epidemic of worldwide concern. On July 20, the Centers for Disease Control reported 3,106,932 cases of COVID, with 59,260 new cases and a total of 132,855 deaths, 799 of those deaths on that day alone.

News reports from March 19, 2020, told the story of a church gathering in a Navajo community that led to an outbreak of the novel coronavirus, which church members then spread in their communities when they returned home to the western side on the Navajo Nation after the service. Christianity has long been a vector distributing destruction in Indian Country. And outbreak emerged in the infamous "drunk tank," or Detoxification Center, in the bordertown of Gallup, New Mexico. The hospital and the detox personnel released infected patients without a quarantine plan, and the outbreak spread through the town and into nearby native communities.

On April 10, COVID-19 cases on tribal lands were more than four times the rate in the United States. By May 18, rates of infection on the Navajo Nation surpassed all the states, including New York, which had been the pandemic's epicenter. On June 26, in South Dakota, Native peoples made up half of confirmed cases of the coronavirus. There are a number of reasons for this. Native peoples are at a higher risk from infectious disease, because they are subjects of settler conquest, which produces geographical isolation, limited health care access, high poverty levels, and a prevalence of diabetes and other preexisting conditions. They also stole crucial resources like water to facilitate the growth of their cities and bordertowns. By July, the fifth month, a second wave of the disease surged. The virus, for which there was no effective treatment or cure, has become the source of political division during the first and second waves. In the US, death and disease disproportionately affect communities of color, which have suffered the highest infection and death rates.

Tribal nations followed the Centers for Disease Control's guidelines and enacted some of the strictest measures of safety and protection, even as they battled with the federal government for funding to address the spread of the virus. In New Mexico and Arizona counties with significant Native and Navajo populations, Native leaders closed roads to their communities and enacted weekday curfews and weekend lockdowns in efforts to slow the spread of the virus. The public offered money, food, water, and personal protection supplies as part of the relief effort.

Cities, bordertowns, and state governments dominated by Christian whites bizarrely called for a faith-based approach to combating the virus. They confronted those who took protective measures, such as wearing a mask in public, with physical and verbal assaults, and these efforts stymied Native nations' science-based efforts to halt the pandemic. Approximately 70 percent of Native people live off designated Native nations, and many find themselves in settler bordertowns hostile to public health. Settlers used the pandemic, as settlers use all pandemics, to whip up anti-Indian hatred.

Native peoples live in worlds remade by settler pandemics. In the 1918 pandemic, only 85 of the 140 people at San Ildefonso, in the Southwest, survived. In many places, deaths were not recorded, so the numbers are unknown.[12] Upon their arrival into the "New World," the carriers of the smallpox brought death to about 90 percent of the Native population, from which the Native peoples never recovered. If this is to be the last settler pandemic, it will be because Native and Black organizers and activists, the great destroyers of settler society, have joined in solidarity to confront the racial oppression at the heart of all settler relations.[13]

Public Health

Native people:

- are 50 percent more likely than others to have a substance use disorder;
- are 60 percent more likely to commit suicide;
- are twice as likely to die during childbirth;
- are three times more likely to die from diabetes;
- are five times more likely to die from tuberculosis;
- die on average five years sooner than other Americans;[14]
- have 50 percent less access to Indian Health Service (IHS) care if they are low-income and uninsured, which is the majority of Native people.[15]

This is not public health. These statistics describe an ongoing war against Native people. War, as we know, is profitable. Health care in settler societies, particularly the United States, is not organized around public health or the well-being of humanity but, instead, around profit. And this leaves Native people without health care forced to rely on the IHS or rundown urgent care clinics in reservation bordertowns.

Even if health care is nominally available to Native people, many avoid it. They are tired of the racism and the discrimination; tired of being pathologized as addicts or state-supported freeloaders. For poor and unsheltered Native people, entry into an emergency room or clinic for treatment often results in arrest and incarceration because of petty violations or intoxication. In the bordertown of Albuquerque, New Mexico, you will find more cops than nurses pacing the hallways of hospitals. Native youth report being apprehended by child welfare or incarcerated in mental health facilities against their will, simply because they sought care at a medical facility. It's common for Native people to be turned away or manipulated into receiving treatments like sterilization or tooth extraction, because IHS facilities are too understaffed or underfunded to provide a broad spectrum of adequate care. This is compounded by the long history of colonial food technologies, such as withholding food rations and the scorched earth campaigns, that have created a chronic lack of access to nutritious food.

The result of all this is that Native people have a profound and enduring mistrust of the health care system. And when we are unwell, we would often rather live with the pain (or die) than deal with a racist institution that violates our bodies and our sovereignty whenever we have to cross a threshold into an IHS clinic or a hospital. Health care should be free, competent, and respectful of everyone, not the least of all Native people whose homelands these private and state facilities occupy.

CHAPTER FOUR

Looting

Settler Colonialism

Colonialism refers to territorial expansion by which European settlers established legal, political, and economic domination over people and territory throughout Asia, Africa, and the Americas, beginning in the sixteenth century. Colonialism is the spatial diffusion of capitalist relations across the globe. It is a mode of domination characterized by the brutal repression of Native peoples and the transformation of local economies and infrastructure to serve colonial interests "at home." The version of colonialism referred to as "settler colonialism" includes the seizure of land, the violent destruction of an existing Native society, and the creation of a permanent settler society on stolen land. There is no "postcolonialism" in settler colonialism. It is intended as an invasion that *never ends*.

Settlers intend to eliminate Natives in order to replace them, a process that is, Patrick Wolfe explains, "never far" from the question of genocide. Settler colonial elimination targets humans and other than humans (such as destruction of the buffalo and the environment) and has a beginning but no end. The elimination of the Native takes many forms, all of which must be understood as endorsed by law. This is what Wolfe means when he calls settler invasion a structure. Through legal practice and the violence work of vigilantism, bordertown police, laws, and legal practices, settler colonialism includes the seizure of Native land, the arresting of Native life, the suspension of Native cultural practices, the upending of Native sovereignty, and the conversion of Native peoples into criminals.

"The story of the new world is horror," writes Chickasaw scholar Jodi Byrd. "The story of America a crime," she continues. And, if this is so, then settler law and order trample the crime scene that colonialism leaves.[1] "Within the narrative practices of nation formation, laws that regulate Native status and rights," Lenape scholar Joanne Barker argues, "are central in defining the conditions of power for those classified as 'white.' These laws have worked so concertedly over time to normalize the legal, social, and economic positions of privilege for 'whites' over Native lands, resources, and bodies that those classified as white have come not only to feel entitled to their privileges and benefits under the law—in fact, expecting the law to continue protecting those privileges and benefits— but also to enjoy the right to exclude them from nonwhites."[2]

But settler colonialism presents a paradox. While it thrives in Australia, Canada, Israel, New Zealand, and the United States, it fails, according to Audra Simpson, "at what it is supposed to do: eliminate Native people; take all their land; absorb them into a white, property-owning body politic."[3] How should we explain colonialism's failure at its only stated purpose?

We might begin by noting that the settler state does not recognize it as a failure. To the settler state, it is only a matter of time. The history of the settler state is not a story of the violent settler domination of Native people, rather it is a story of settler sovereignty and Indian depravity, of settler civilization and Native savagery. Frantz Fanon described colonialism as a form of "pure violence" in which "the police and military ensure the colonized are kept under close scrutiny and contained by rifle butts and napalm."[4] But the pure violence of settler colonialism requires the constant reproduction of the conditions for that violence as legitimate, productive, and righteous. According to Sherene Razack, settler colonial violence tells a story "of the Indian on the brink of death ... a narrative of the vanishing Indian that has been dear to white settler societies from the time of their inception. Inundating us with details of fatty livers, mental illness, alcoholic belligerence and a mysterious incapacity to cope with modern life, legal records tell the story of a pre-modern people encountering and losing out to a more advanced and superior race."[5] The presence of Native people challenges the legitimacy of the settler project, and so the settler state responds with a story of Indians as a "dying race," as suspended between life and death. They are "the kind of human one can only deal with through force." The violent deaths of Native people in settler states is so common as to be unexceptional. In Saskatoon, Saskatchewan, Canadian police abandon Native men and women to freeze to death on the frozen tundra. In bordertowns like Gallup, New Mexico, and Rapid City, South Dakota, Native people are left to freeze to death in the winter, to die ingloriously in their own homelands. The violence of the settler colonial state against the Native is depicted as a purifying violence, a violence that releases the Native from her subjugation, in which "killing becomes saving, and murder brings redemption."[6]

The very presence of Native people marks a disorder in the settler state, and this requires violence. Violence, in particular state violence, is part of everyday life for Native people in settler society, but, despite this, police and settlers are never "responsible" for taking Native lives, because the Native is the impossible subject in the settler state. And the settler story of the "vanishing Indian" provides a ready-made alibi.

Rape

Two Amnesty International reports, *Stolen Sisters* and *Maze of Injustice*, brought global attention to what Native women have been reporting for decades: they suffer disproportionately from physical and emotional abuse, sexual assaults, and rapes compared to other women in the United States and Canada. A 1996 Canadian government report revealed that Native women between the ages of twenty-five and forty-four, were five times more likely than all other women of the same age to die as the result of violence. In the US, reports show that Native American and Alaska Native women are more than 2.5 times more like to be raped or sexually assaulted than other women in the US, and that nearly 35 percent of American Indian and Alaska Native women—more than one in three—will be raped during their lifetime. The comparable figure for the US as a whole is less than one in five. Native women suffer from these rates of violence because they are Native women.[7] This is true everywhere, particularly in bordertown cities. The Urban Indian Health Institute examined the patterns of missing and murdered Native women and girls in seventy-one cities and found the same patterns of sexual violence.[8]

In her study *The Beginning and End of Rape*, Sarah Deer lays out the reasons that Native women as victims of rape cannot expect to see justice. They are hesitant to report to authorities, because they are often revictimized by a system that still does not recognize the rape of Native women as wrong. On and off Native nations, law enforcement remains indifferent, because rape is considered a major crime that falls under the jurisdiction of the federal government. For this reason, rape charges are often declined, and perpetrators go free. Victims often feel ashamed, so there remains a silence about rape experiences.[9] As Deer notes, rape affects not just an individual victim but the entire community. "Sovereignty thus suffers when the women suffer."[10]

The 1994 Violence Against Women Act, amended and reauthorized three times, most recently in 2013, intended to confront violence by funding, programming, and seeking criminal justice reform and included resources for tribal domestic violence and sexual abuse. The 2005 reauthorization of VAWA was amended with Title IX, which addressed violence against Native women specifically. However, the 2011 Violence Against Women's Act was deemed controversial, because it included provisions about Native women, immigrants, and the LGBTQI2S community, leading to a stalemate until President Obama signed it into law on March 7, 2013. A key provision that caused white consternation was fear that a Native nation might hold a non-Indian perpetrator accountable for violence against Native women and other victims. Thus, VAWA 2013 limits a Native nation's ability to prosecute a non-Indian to ones who have "sufficient ties to the nation."[11] VAWA 2013 only partially addresses rape on designated Native nations and does not cover women who live in urban spaces or gender nonconforming individuals.

Sexual assaults of Native women continue to be of dire concern, exacerbated by ongoing exploitation of natural resources like fracking. Gas and oil mining near and on tribal lands has increased attacks on Native women by male workers who live in man camps. In the two-hundred-thousand-square-mile Bakken region between Montana and North Dakota, as fracking increased so did the reports of sexual assaults of Native women. In fracking fields alongside the eastern boundary of the Navajo Nation, similar reports emerged about rates of sexual assault of Diné women who live in communities near man camps.[12] Tribal authorities have no jurisdiction in these spaces, and even if they did, their record for protecting women has been dismal.

Native feminists have explained a settler tradition of rape as integral to conquest of the land and of Native people. In European and then American societies, men enforced women's subordination to men. They imported this logic of patriarchy to Native lands. Early settler documents attest to the rape of Native women as settlers warred against Native people. Indeed, settler common sense dictates that Native women's bodies are inherently "dirty" and, thus, "rapable." As Native feminists note, Native women's bodies are treated as violently as the land is, for women's bodies are Mother Earth.[13]

Once Native people had been militarily defeated and reduced to spaces called reservations, the sexual assaults at the forts by US soldiers continued in boarding school spaces from the late nineteenth century into the twentieth century. Colonizers have long tried to denigrate Native peoples as less than human. A key way they have done this has been through the rape of Native women. Native nations and communities cannot prosper until the rape of women, children, and LGBTQI2S relatives is addressed in ways that reaffirm kinship as the network that offers support for victims and refuses rape as the normal order of the world.

Man Camp

At an April 2019 public meeting on resource exploitation in Santa Fe, New Mexico, Congresswoman Deb Haaland posed what some considered an outrageous question. Are oil and gas workers soliciting Navajo women and girls for sex? The New Mexico Oil and Gas Association, an industry lobbying group, joined a number of conservative commentators to condemn Haaland for asking the question. No one answered her question.

Oil and gas have long been an important economic driver in New Mexico, but fracking technologies and new discoveries in the Permian Basin and San Juan Basin over the past decade, along with a number of pipelines, have transformed New Mexico into one of the largest oil and gas producers in the United States. The boom has brought thousands of workers to New Mexico, most in semipermanent settlements throughout southern and northwestern New Mexico. These man camps, as they are known, are temporary housing communities set up for the well-paid, typically male workers employed in the lucrative oil and gas industry.

Navajo communities lie within the San Juan Basin, a major fracking region, and adjacent to the camps, which come and go with the "boom-and-bust" cycle common to oil and gas production in the American West. During boom times, man camps proliferate everywhere. During the bust cycle, they just as quickly disappear, leaving behind polluted landscapes. These are camps primarily populated by young single men with no ties to local communities. They bring with them an increase in physical and sexual violence, including rape, sexual assault, sexual assault of minors, and sex trafficking in nearby communities.

We find man camps throughout the United States. As Patina Park, executive director of the Minnesota Indian Women's Resource Center said in opposition to man camps in her community, "Violence against our earth and water is perpetrated on a daily basis, against those things absolutely vital to our very existence," adding, "We can't be surprised that people who would rape our land are also raping our people."

The discovery of high-grade oil shale in the Bakken region of North Dakota, for example, brought thousands of mostly male workers to the land adjacent to the Fort Berthold Indian Reservation. Between 2006 and 2012, the rate of violence by oil and gas workers against Native women, particularly aggravated assault, increased 70 percent from before the boom. In contrast, there was no corresponding rise of violent crime in the counties outside of the Bakken oil region. Reports of violent victimization in non-Bakken counties were down 8 percent during the same time period. Rates of violent crimes such as homicide, nonnegligent manslaughter, rape and sexual assault, robbery, and aggravated assault increased 30 percent in the Bakken region. Settlers hire more cops when they see numbers like these. We seek an end to this violence only when settler society comes to an end.

Related to the tar sands region of Alberta and the US Bakken region of North Dakota, Canada's federal government released its Missing and Murdered Native Women and Girls report, in which it called missing and murdered Native women an epidemic of state-induced genocide. In the findings presented in the 1,200-page document, the Canadian government linked extractive industries and man camps to the violence against Native women.

On April 21, 2015, a coalition of Native American and women's organizations filed a submission to the United Nations Expert Mechanism on the Rights of Native Peoples, requesting UN intervention in the epidemic of sexual violence brought on by extreme fossil fuel extraction in the Great Lakes and Great Plains region. The coalition explicitly documents the connection between extreme extraction and sexual violence against Native women in the Bakken oil region and the tar sands region of Alberta, Canada, and directly connects the violence of the man camps to the history of colonization, genocide, and systemic gendered violence against Native peoples. As UN special rapporteur James Anaya explained, "Indigenous women have reported that the influx of workers into Native communities as a result of extractive projects also led to increased incidents of sexual harassment and violence, including rape and assault."

The arrival of the virus that causes COVID-19 in New Mexico in 2020 marked the beginning of a bust cycle for oil and gas exploitation in and around Navajo communities along the fracking corridor. This reveals another pattern common in settler bordertowns. Settlers come in many guises. Sometimes they bring their men, and sometimes they bring their diseases—sometimes they bring both.

Treaty

Native peoples express kinship through their relationships to the land and with all beings, human and other than human. This kinship links the past, present, and future. It is through treaties that Native nations enter into formal kinship relations with other nations, including settler nations, animal nations, and other Native nations. Native people have long negotiated and agreed to treaties with the expectation that parties to treaties will respect and honor them, with a mutual goal to create peaceful coexistence and harmony. It was with such an understanding that the Council of Three Fires (Anishinaabe, Odawa, Potawatomi), the Haudenosaunee (Iroquois) Six Nations (Cayuga, Mohawk, Oneida, Onondaga, Seneca, Tuscarora), the Lenape Clans and Nations, and the Muscogee (Creek) Confederacy of more than sixty nations and towns entered into treaty relationships with the US government.

Given this definition of treaties, it is fair to say that European and American governments did not enter into treaty relationships with Native nations. Before the birth of the United States in 1776, European nations negotiated agreements with Native nations. These were not treaties of respect but, rather, treaties designed to establish the conditions for Native elimination, which is the organizing principle of settler society. Between 1722 and 1774, Native leaders faced impossible choices. How should they confront the extreme violence of settler culture? Should they stand and fight against great odds (many did) or make concessions by allying with colonizer factions? Settler squatters followed traders, forts, and land speculators in an endless onslaught of greed for land and resources. Treaties with settler governments required equally endless land cessions. Native nations received their own concessions in treaties, but these never lasted long. Often before the ink dried on the documents, settlers appropriated more Native lands, thereby violating the agreements. For example, settlers violated the Treaty of New York, signed with the Muscogee Nation in 1790, by immediately squatting on remaining Muscogee lands.

The United States loved to enter into treaties with Native nations, since this facilitated recognition of its fledgling stature among other nations. The US Constitution mentions Native nations in Article One, Section Eight, making clear that Congress shall have the power to "regulate commerce with foreign nations, and among the several states, and with the Indian tribes." The US Constitution holds that once a treaty is signed by the president and ratified by the Senate, it becomes the "supreme law of the land." The fact that the US government broke every treaty it entered into with Native nations tells you all you need to know about settler law.

There is a bureaucracy to this treaty-making. The Office of Indian Affairs, established in 1824 as part of the Department of War, negotiated treaties with Native nations. Twenty-five years later, this responsibility became the purview of the Department of the Interior, which perhaps indicates that the US government considered the Indian Wars complete. While treaty-making with Native nations was ended in 1872 by an act of Congress, settler land speculation continued. The 1887 General Allotment Act opened millions of acres of Native land for settlers. This continued through various congressional acts. The formation of National Forests required the theft of Native lands for the establishment of eminent domain. The relocation acts of the 1950s forced Native families from their homelands.

The entity known as the United States is consistent. It has signed more than five hundred treaties with Native nations and has not honored a single one. Settler historians and intellectuals carry on the spirit of their ancestors by denying the sovereignty of Native nations, deeming them "domestic dependent nations." By contrast, Native leaders and their people relay a consciousness across generations, from ancestors to relatives, that travels by memory and through kinship with the land. For Native peoples, treaties represent a commitment to kinship and continue to serve as acts of diplomacy and evidence of a long-standing status of Native nationhood. Sovereign nations enter into treaties with other sovereign nations not domestic populations.[14] Settler nations enter into treaties to steal land.

Law

All law of the liberal capitalist state is class law. It claims for itself the privileged objectivity necessary to adjudicate social conflict in ways deemed just by the liberal capitalist state. Let's not be confused. What is considered *just* by the liberal capitalist state is what is understood to be instrumental to the liberal capitalist state. Whatever is *just* is whatever preserves property relations. To do this, but in a way presented as universal and objective, law depicts society as comprised of equal subjects. Do not be fooled. Law's seemingly objective nonviolent authority is always established through the uneven and unequal application of violence. Law's violence is visible to all those who refuse its authority. It remains invisible, or acceptable when not hidden, to all those whose interests it serves.

Law, therefore, is not objective and has no meaning outside of the specific political and economic conditions it helps bring to life and ruthlessly sustains. For this reason, any effort to critically understand law must begin by understanding the context in which it operates. One way that law presents itself as objective and, therefore, just is by presenting itself free from the relations it serves and the adjectives that condition it. Law, in other words, is never only law. For example, it is through class law, presented simply *as* law, that the state defends the unjust division of the conditions that make life possible. You own land and have great wealth. You own nothing and have only your labor to sell. This is so, because class law, as law, defines it as such. What is clearly unjust becomes just through the application of law. And what is violent—class law—becomes nonviolent when simply rendered as law.

What about law in settler colonial society? In all settler states, law is always and only the law of the settler, never of the Native. Consider the Marshall Trilogy, the three US Supreme Court cases that establish law's defense of US settler colonialism—*Johnson v. McIntosh*, 21 US 543 (1823); *Cherokee Nation v. Georgia*, 30 US 1 (1831); and *Worcester v. Georgia*, 31 US 515 (1832). In *Johnson*, the Court relied on the Doctrine of Discovery, the guiding principle of imperial expansion that posits imperial conquest as the legitimate legal origins of property. In *Johnson*, the Supreme Court staked its settler claim to Native land and rejected a claim to property based on the argument that Native people could only convey property to the US sovereign. The European "discovery" of lands that would later become the United States established the very concept of *legal property*, and, thus, Native peoples in what became the United States had no right or claim to property. The next two cases established Indian tribes as domestic dependent nations of the US sovereign, a legal formulation that limits Native sovereignty to one conditioned by and subservient to US national sovereignty. It is doctrinal, which to the settler lawyer means that there ain't no getting around it. All law in the United States is settler law. The US Supreme Court established Native tribes as equal under a law that deems them perpetually unequal.

Among law's many obfuscations, including those described above, is its claim to nonviolence. Law demands an obedience to what it claims is legal. By doing so, it displaces responsibility for its violence. In other words, the violence that law requires to enforce the relations that law claims are just must always be called something other than violence. Law sentences a woman to death, orders a man to prison, issues a warrant to evict a family from its home, and law calls this justice; a parent steals bread for a hungry child, a woman kills a battering spouse, a family squats in an abandoned home, and law calls this violence.

Only the settler and property owner can look to the law for justice, and only the settler and property owner receives it. Settler law cannot be the basis for Native liberation.

Alcohol

Alcohol lies at the heart of the relationship between Native people and settlers. We find alcohol distribution to Native peoples by settlers at the first colonial encounters. The introduction of alcohol facilitated the exchange of Native lands and trade items, including animal pelts and woven textiles, and as exchange for sex with Native women. Alcohol was often introduced to Native leaders negotiating treaties, who, plied with liquor until drunk, signed away massive tracts of land. As a temperance tract put it, "The trader took his pelts, the settler took his land, and whiskey did not last long."[15]

The firewater myth holds that Native people are more susceptible to alcohol's intoxicating affects, because "they can't hold their liquor," or that they're biologically or genetically predisposed to alcoholism, because "they haven't built up a tolerance." In this scenario, colonization doesn't condition the use of alcohol, genes do.

The introduction of alcohol, alongside the onslaught of invasion, war, and genocide, had traumatic effects on Native peoples, but the 1633 decree by the General Court of Massachusetts that made the trade in alcohol illegal ("no man shall sell or give any strong water to an Indian") depicted the problem as a cultural and biological one, not a consequence of colonial violence. The nascent colonies enacted prohibitions of alcohol sales to Indians continuing to 1802, when US president Thomas Jefferson signed an act controlling the distribution and sale of alcohol to Native people.

Native nations also policed alcohol use as part of their treaties with the United States and as an assertion of sovereignty to curtail its abuse as a notorious tactic used by traders, especially in the bordertowns. In 1819, as a response to liquor sales to Indians, the Cherokees enacted the first prohibition law with a fine of $100 for the offender. The Choctaw treaty of 1820 included a provision that regulated liquor traffic, insisted upon by the Native peoples themselves. Between 1832 and 1892, Congress took various actions to halt liquor sales to Indians. These early prohibition efforts were eventually repealed when the US government ended prohibition on the sale of liquor to Native peoples. However, on Native lands, tribal governments still outlaw liquor sales and use. Thus, the bordertown became a space where Native peoples congregated to buy and drink alcohol.

Native nations outlaw the possession and consumption of alcohol on their lands, which has the effect of promoting bordertown drinking. Native drinking in bordertowns, therefore, is always "public" drinking, which creates the conditions for all the policing of Native drinking that follows. This is always based on the myth of the drunk Indian. The settler always sees alcohol through a racial lens. White middle-class and affluent settlers drink "socially" and freely access services for alcohol abuse (which they consider a disease). Drinking by Native people, on the other hand, represents a deep cultural and biological pathology that settlers respond to with ruthless criminal enforcement. This strong stigma attached to Indian drinking remains to this day in settler society, and even in Native communities. The Native temperance movement emerged from this myth.

The history of this myth and the development of this pathology of Indian drinking is a history of the legal and scientific construction of the drunk Indian. In a 1953 report that surveyed the living conditions of Indians in places like Gallup, Farmington, Cortez, Flagstaff, and other towns adjacent to the Navajo Nation, researchers cited Native alcohol use as the greatest cause of disorderly conduct in bordertowns. The report also alleged that a majority of those cited by law enforcement for alcohol-related crimes came off the reservation and into bordertowns.[16] In other words, Native people who drank became the racial trope for any kind of breach of the social and legal contract of civility that settlers who drink supposedly abided by.

By the 1970s, activists confronted these alcohol-soaked bordertowns, targeting the laws and politics of alcohol sales that contributed to patterns of bordertown violence. Their relatives were dying from alcohol-related diseases, with easy access and the culture of public use leading to exposure deaths, domestic violence, and vehicular homicides. "Alcohol-related" became a catch-all adjective to describe any sort of violence or death. Activists testified in front of civil rights commissions and held protests to point out that Native peoples' lives mattered less than the profits that local white and Hispano elites could make from selling alcohol to Native people. Alcohol has always been a tool of exploitation and Native erasure.

Capitalism

Capitalism is an economic system organized around the private ownership of the means of production (land, resources, money) and the private control of the wealth produced by wage laborers. In its first instantiation, capitalism required force in the form of police and military violence to establish "the reformation, by juridical means, of relations of authority and service that had been previously ensured by the customary bonds of the serf to his manor and the labourer to his master."[17] Capitalism relies on law and police as the "instrument by which the people's land is stolen."[18] As Karl Marx explained, capitalism arrives dripping with blood: "Agricultural folk first forcibly expropriated from the soil, driven from their homes, turned into vagabonds, and then whipped, branded and tortured."[19] This was as true in England when Marx was writing, as it was in Standing Rock while we were writing.

The enduring contradiction of capitalism is that its antagonists, the working poor, are also its lifeblood. "As bourgeois social relations began to stamp themselves across the face of society the major threat appeared to be the laboring poor."[20] Managing the simmering animosities and hostile antagonisms between the ruling class and this exploited poor was and remains capitalism's primary preoccupation. Capitalists look to the state to manage the poor, because capitalist prosperity is impossible without poverty. After all, there is no wealth to accumulate without a laboring poor forced to sell its labor to survive. The working class "is just as much an appendage of capital as the lifeless instruments of labor are."[21]

But there are differences. The hammer will not run away. The factory belt will not demand higher wages. There's no chance the trucks in the fleet will conspire to overthrow the bosses. But the capitalist and, thus, the liberal capitalist state must take "good care to prevent the workers, those instruments of production who are possessed of consciousness, from running away."[22]

Accumulation requires a pool of cheap and readily available labor power—a relative surplus population of a laboring poor—that can be "constantly hunted down" and put to work.[23] If you have ever worked for a wage, you are a member of a population that is always potentially surplus. You might be part of a "floating" population, forever chasing and sometimes finding work in an industry that constantly shifts its labor needs and requirements. You might be part of a "latent" population, joining great migrations of labor from the reservation to the bordertown, from a dying industry to a new one, or from the Global South to the North. And God help you if you are part of a "stagnant" population," what Marx called an "active labour army," maintained by capital and patrolled by police as an "inexhaustible reservoir of disposable labour-power" where the conditions of life "sink below the average normal level of the working class."[24] Those who fall into the "stagnant" population work the most but make the least. At the margins of this army, you find yourself in "the sphere of pauperism" and vagrancy, joined by the "demoralized, the ragged, and those unable to work . . . the mutilated, the sickly, the widows, etc."[25] If you are Native, you find yourself under the thumb of the settler state and its professional Indian killers, the police. It is the job of settler police to patrol the poor, to be the occupying army in the bordertown. When police "looked at beggars and vagrants, they saw able-bodied (but lazy, ignorant and potentially rebellious) workers withholding their labour and thus not producing wealth."[26] This is the threat of poverty that police manage. Police are part of this enormous science of capitalist logistics.

Capitalism needs colonialism and racism. "The need of a constantly expanding market for its products chases the bourgeoisie over the entire surface of the globe. It must nestle everywhere, settle everywhere, establish connexions everywhere."[27] Capitalism is always on the hunt for resources and markets and relies on institutions like bordertown police in this hunt. Bordertown police is not an institution apart from this project. The job of police is to hunt. Police is "a hunting institution, the state's arm for pursuit, entrusted by it with tracking, arresting, imprisoning."[28]

Colonial domination establishes the conditions and relations of racial capitalism in which Black, Brown, and Native suffering and death serve settler and class interests.[29] "Dividing, hunting, terrorizing, those were the principles of a good colonial government."[30] Racial differentiation has always been a fundamental mechanism that capital puts to work to forge and enforce the "color lines" and "property lines" of racial capitalism.[31] Capitalism and its adjunct liberal state cannot exist without mechanisms to racially differentiate between those groups that threaten "good order" and those groups that uphold it. Capitalism cannot exist without a state willing and able to defend the wage relation, private property, settler police violence, and the Native dispossession that characterize all of these.

Bordertown Political Economy

On May 1, 2020, the bordertown of Gallup, New Mexico, enacted a city-wide lockdown, invoking the state's Riot Control Act to restrict entry into the city in an effort to quell the skyrocketing numbers of COVID-19 infections in surrounding McKinley County. This decision came shortly after reports emerged about the Navajo Nation having the third highest COVID-19 infection rate after New York and New Jersey (a little under a month later, the Navajo Nation climbed to first place). According to the 2010 census, Native people comprise 70 percent of McKinley County's overall population (white people comprise 16 percent) and 44 percent of Gallup's population (compared to 34 percent white).[32] The majority of these people are Diné, or Navajo.

Who was Gallup protecting itself from? While reactions to the lockdown varied, Diné citizens of the Navajo Nation understood the message loud and clear: Gallup wants Navajo money, but it doesn't want Navajo people, especially those contagious with colonialism. Many were outraged by the anti-Indian racism behind the lockdown, which kept businesses open for Navajo commerce but restricted the free movement of Navajo people in and out of the city and reservation, despite the fact that Gallup is surrounded by Navajo communities and sits on customary and ancestral Navajo land. A protest sign erected on Highway 491—the major thoroughfare between the Navajo Nation and Gallup—read, "STOP Giving Gallup $$$! They Profit from our Deaths." "They profit from our deaths." This phrase encapsulates bordertown political economies in a nutshell.

Bordertowns are economic hubs for Native people who have no choice but to shop in these racist settlements because of the lack of infrastructure on reservations. Bordertown economies rely almost entirely on Native customers to turn a profit. While these businesses would collapse without Native dollars and cheap Native labor (something we've seen due to the COVID-19 pandemic), almost no bordertown businesses are owned by Native people. Why is this? Pawnshops, car dealerships, payday loan shops, trading posts, retail stores, and liquor stores all rely on a business model that exploits Native people for their money, labor, talents, and culture. In other words, the political economy of bordertowns extracts value from Native people for the benefit of settler wealth and comfort. This process of extraction and exploitation feeds the larger project of settler colonialism, because it facilitates the accumulation of power in the hands of settlers. This accumulation depends on the diminishment of Native life.

Native workers are routinely exploited for their cultural and artistic labor, which serves as a major source of profits for traders and pawnshop brokers who mark up items to sell to non-Native tourists seeking their "Indian experience." In fact, it is well known that in Gallup legacy trader families make profits in the millions of dollars off of Native-made jewelry, textiles, and artwork. Bordertowns like Santa Fe, New Mexico, one of the most popular tourist destinations in the world, owe their popularity and profitability to their proximity to and marketing of Native culture. Although euphemistically termed the *arts and crafts* industry, this type of tourism-driven economy actually exploits Native labor for the benefit of wealthy gallery owners, traders, and collectors. Moreover, the image of culture and tradition that drives the Native art market in bordertowns like Gallup and Santa Fe is meant to respond to the tastes of settler consumers, who prefer to interact with Native people through the nonthreatening act of buying and fetishizing objects, rather than confronting the ongoing impact of settler colonialism on Native life. Recent settler outrage in Santa Fe about how decolonial graffiti on monuments of conquest ruins the beauty of the city demonstrates the depth of settlers' desire for a Pueblo Disneyland experience where Native people don't openly challenge settler entitlement. When confronted, settler tourists and business owners become violent, as was the case recently in Gallup when white and Hispano business owners—many of them traders of Native art and culture—armed themselves against Native youth marching in solidarity with Black Lives Matter.

And we can't forget liquor establishments. As Larry Casuse pointed out, many of the liquor establishments in Gallup—the number of which exceeds the legal limit of establishments per capita according to New Mexico state law—are owned by the families of local Hispano political elites. The stores are highly lucrative for their owners. Tourism and liquor sales exploit Native misery and desperation to net millions for local settler elites. Native people are expected to produce value, but when they object to their exploitation they are quickly silenced through violence. Money and commodities are granted a privilege to freely cross borders that most of humanity doesn't enjoy.

In addition to these types of commodity-driven businesses is the extractive industry. Oil and gas pipelines and railways that transport coal are common sights in bordertowns. Resources travel through bordertowns on their way from mines located within reservation boundaries to processing plants that feed energy to mega-settlements like Phoenix, Los Angeles, and Denver. Just as often, the resources are processed—in addition to being mined—in plants on reservations, which in the case of the Navajo Nation are *all* located next to bordertowns where extractive industry workers (and executives) live. This leads to the shadow economies of bordertowns: sex work, drugs, and human trafficking. The majority of workers in these sectors are also Native, and they typically serve settler workers, many of whom work in coal plants and fracking fields, as is the case in the bordertown of Farmington, New Mexico. Bordertowns are the original man camps. Sex work, drugs, and slavery were indispensable to frontier economies where settlers worked to consolidate US empire and turn a fortune on the privatization and enclosure of dispossessed Native land. These practices continue to this day.

Class

In his 1889 essay "The Gospel of Wealth," Andrew Carnegie, a notorious nineteenth-century robber baron, defined the problem of wealth not as gross inequality and outright theft but as a failure to create a "harmonious relationship" between rich and poor. The disparity between the mansions of millionaires and the shacks of laborers, Carnegie wrote, "is not to be deplored"—but should be embraced as progress. After visiting "the Sioux," Carnegie concluded that "Indians are today where civilized man then was," when class rule did not exist. "Neither master nor servant," he warned, "was as well situated then as today. A relapse to old conditions would be disastrous to both—not the least to him [sic] who serves—and would sweep away civilization with it."[33]

For Carnegie, a class-based society marks civilizational progress forged in the destruction of Native and noncapitalist societies. In settler societies, class emerged from Native land theft and elimination, which continue to uphold all other social and class positions. The removal of European peasants from the land by wealthy Europeans created a new "free" laboring class at the same time as European invaders were dispossessing Native people of their lands and expanding the institution of African slavery. This stock of landless peasants became cannon fodder for the invasion of the Americas—to kill Indians and to own Africans in the service of profit. To neutralize potential conflict between poor and rich settlers, white supremacy, which wasn't invented out of whole cloth but, rather, was constructed by law and made concrete in the act of colonization, became the governing ideology.

For example, the 1862 Homestead Act opened up 270 million acres of Native land—an area the size of California and Texas combined—to 1.6 million mostly poor white settlers at no cost. But before the land could be given away, it had to be wrested away from Native peoples, often with genocidal violence. Of course, Black, Mexican, Asian, and Native peoples were excluded from the benefits of this federal program. Today, 98 percent of private land (856 million acres) in the US is owned by white settlers. This land is worth more than $1 trillion, and a quarter of white settlers alive today directly benefit from the Homestead Act. In a settler society, land equals class mobility. It is also the basis of kinship between white settlers of different classes; land and property resolve class antagonisms and allow poor and working-class white settlers to feel like they own a piece of the American pie. Meanwhile, this gross system has created capitalists like Ted Turner, who owns more than two million acres of land—more land than all of the Native nations combined! And, in 2017, eight powerful capitalists, all white men, owned more wealth than half the planet!

However, the social position "settler" is not a class position but, rather, a position of power created and upheld through law, politics, culture, and society as a whole. Because of class rule, not all settlers are equal. Most white people, for example, are not landowners or capitalists. And the working class is not made up entirely of settlers. Natives and colonized peoples are working-class too. They too were removed from their lands and forced to sell their labor. Lack of awareness about the origins and function of the social position of the "settler," however, prevents solidarities among the working class. As anti-colonial movements the world over have demonstrated, the colonial relation—who stole the land, who works it, how it became a commodity—*is* the capital relation. Anti-colonial struggles are the strongest forms of class struggle. These struggles seek the annihilation of the ruling class *and* the working class, because a classless society subordinates no one group to another. However, decolonization requires the annihilation of the settler's privileged social position and the recuperation of Native nationhood, where classes would cease to exist, and land and wealth would be restored not according to privilege but according to Native relations premised on reciprocity, equality, and justice. Those who refuse to recognize land theft as the primary motor of class war in North America are on the wrong side of that war.

Exploitation

The exploitation of land and labor is foundational to capitalism, an ecological and economic system based on private interest and private gain. The lives of those who work for a living are defined by this exploitation. They work hard, and then harder, long, and then longer, and always for less and less. Corporations use words like *efficiency* and *productivity*, and phrases like *the bottom line* to disguise this exploitation as a social good. But there is no social good to any system based on exploitation.

The only interest of those who control the means of production is private gain, and, therefore, everything they do is an effort to intensify the exploitation of nature and labor. They keep the cost of labor and nature as cheap as possible and as available as possible through all manner of tricks and deceits, structured always by violence and the threat of violence. All this to defend their indefensible right to grow wealthy from the labor of others, to despoil the lands of others, and to take as their own wealth to which they have no legitimate claim.

Their absurd claims make sense within the context of a capitalist system they designed. The bosses, with the help of law and police, determine wages, benefits, and, ultimately, the very livelihoods and destinies of the workers trapped in this arrangement because they have only their labor to sell. Capitalists seek nothing less than total control over markets, life, power, and money through the gross accumulation of value based on the theft of the wealth produced by the workers. This all happens at the expense—literally, the blood, sweat, and tears—of those who labor. We are governed by our enemies.

What does exploitation mean in personal terms? Those of us who come from poor and working-class backgrounds live in a straitjacket tightened by wage labor. We know what it feels like to be exploited by "the man." We share a collective loathing for landlords, bosses, and the cops and courts who sustain them. We struggle to survive from the wages they pay and with the demands they make. We live in constant fear of losing a job we hate. For women and LGBTQI2S workers the wage defines an exploitation that includes endless sexual harassment and homophobia. We live month-to-month, week-to-week, paycheck-to-paycheck. But we have only our labor to sell so we're stuck in these relations. Refuse to suffer along, and they send goons disguised as lawyers to bust our union organizing. With no collective power to demand better wages and working conditions, we slack off, we work to rule. Fuck "the man." We gossip and talk shit about the bosses. We show up late and take long coffee breaks. We steal their lunch from the breakroom. We sit around the table with our families at the end of an exhausting workday venting about how unfair the system is, how it seems that no matter how hard we work, we can never get ahead. We drink and socialize together to form bonds that allow us to cope with our exploitation.

We know the system is rigged. We know that its very existence is itself a declaration of war on our humanity and dignity. We know exploitation is class warfare, so we wage it. In bordertowns, where Native people make up a large proportion of workers, class warfare requires an understanding not only of capitalism but also of settler colonialism. If settler colonialism seeks to eliminate Native people by dispossessing them of land, political authority, and humanity, then the exploitation of Native labor in bordertowns fulfills the insidious designs of both capitalism and settler colonialism. And we know that this extends beyond the bodies of individual Native laborers to the land and water. Uranium, natural gas, coal, copper, water, and even the sun are exploited by corporations in a manner that parallels the exploitation of Native workers.

Bordertowns are hubs for the transport and processing of land and water converted into "natural resources" by corporations. We see sacred lands; they see profit potential in the conversion of nature into electricity, vehicle fuel, and military weaponry. The wealth that capitalists loot through their exploitation of bordertown labor, land, and water contributes to the elimination of Native futures. When these parasites descend on bordertowns they promise economic development through new frontiers in resource exploitation. We are all depicted as naive for refusing their gifts. Most of these "natural resources" are extracted from Native lands, which creates permanent economic inequalities, because Native nations rarely benefit from the profits of extractive enterprise. This makes true sovereignty and self-determination virtually impossible. And the actual techniques used to exploit land and water for financial gain create permanent wastelands out of Native lands, bodies, waters, and nations. Capitalist exploitation kills all the birds with all the stones; it seeks a permanent underclass of Native workers condemned to forever labor in a constant state of exploitation, living precarious lives in ruined homelands.

Yet there is another form of exploitation at work in bordertowns. Sex trafficking and gender-based violence are forms of exploitation that follow the same logics as those above. Sex trafficking trails only drug trafficking as the second most profitable industry in the world, raking in approximately $32 billion annually. As many Native feminists have pointed out, the economic profit from resource exploitation attracts settlers of every kind, including sex traffickers, who seek profits by converting every social relation into a commodity. Sex trafficking, like oil drilling, hydraulic fracturing, and coal mining, relies on wage labor, though slave labor more accurately describes the relation. Native cis and trans girls and women are either kidnapped and forced into sex work as commodities for trade or forced to "choose" to engage in sex work—itself a type of exploited labor—just to make ends meet.

Distinctions between "criminal" or "informal" industry and "legal" or "formal" industry matter little to the Native workers who are exploited in the interest of bosses, usually white men, who seek to maintain a monopoly on power and profit. All exploitation is a crime, whether it be the so-called legal plunder of Native lands, the rape of Native women, or the refusal to pay Native workers a living wage. Liberation will come when we are able to end our exploitation by overthrowing the very systems that create it—capitalism and settler colonialism—and the class of people who uphold it—corporations, owners, and politicians.

Resource Colonization

Colonization is nothing if not about the extraction of mineral wealth and the exploitation of people. All of this is about resources, particularly what the settler calls natural resources. But beware of some who write about resource colonization. At its best, work on resource colonialism demonstrates the profound destruction at the heart of settler colonialism. At its worst, however, it is a phrase that limits a discussion or analysis of settler colonialism by an abstraction called "resources." Resource colonialism, rendered this way, directs our attention away from histories and contemporary practices and patterns of settler colonialism and instead places its focus on a very limited—and abstract—set of concerns. It is the corporations and non-Native political and economic elites, along with their Native collaborators, and the way these people and institutions conspire to remove authority over the use of something called "resources" from Native people that are of interest to "resource colonization."

There is a very specific political and material effect that follows when we modify "colonization" by the adjective "resource." If the problem is "resource colonization" and not simply "colonization," then the solution is a resolution to the problems defined by the adjective "resource," not one defined by "colonization" more generally. Let's say we're talking about the exploitation of oil and gas or coal or uranium on Native land. Resource colonization draws attention to the non-Native corporations accommodated by the settler state that control and profit from the extraction of oil and gas or coal or uranium. The solution to this problem is not the restoration of Native sovereignty and the abolition of extraction and exploitation and the environmental destruction that follows these processes but, rather, the abolition of the non-Native control of this exploitation. This is not to say that a challenge to the non-Native control of Native land does not constitute a problem for the settler state, rather, it is to say that the phrase *resource colonization* confronts the settler state on its own terms and in ways the settler state is fully equipped to respond to. Consider the US Bureau of Indian Affairs. It has an office of Indian Energy and Economic Development in its Native American Business Development division. What is this if not a way to resolve the central critique of "resource colonization"—that exploitation isn't controlled by Native people or institutions?

But what good can come from a critique of the phrase *resource colonization*? After all, resource colonization defines a history in which persistent underdevelopment came to those tribal nations targeted by resource extraction firms, whether for their water, timber, oil and gas, or uranium. The benefits of this extraction have been enjoyed by the firms that control it and the white settlements that convert these resources into energy. Resource colonization names a version of Native sovereignty now permanently dependent on a resource economy based on exploitation. One genealogy of the phrase *resource colonialism* emerges from this history.

The phrase *resource colonization* depicts extraction as *the* source of underdevelopment. This implies that decolonization struggles should focus on the abolition of resource colonization to make Native development possible. But the very idea of *development*, a term invented by the capitalist nation-state, requires allegiance to all that makes settler colonialism possible—private property, settler and class law, and the liberal state. Decolonization requires more than the abolition of resource colonization; it requires the abolition of the world that makes it possible.

Structural Violence

What is violence? When we think of violence, we often think of physical violence only. A person assaulting and harming another person. Two people fighting. Wars between nations. Can we expand our notion of violence to include social relations and structures of authority and power? Consider structural power enacted through racism, colonialism, capitalism, and heterosexism. These "isms" are part of the fabric of American life; they structure our entire world. Are these "isms" also a form of violence?

Protests erupted after police murdered George Floyd in Minneapolis in late May 2020. Black Lives Matter (BLM) protestors took to the streets to demand an end to police violence, and this demand was not only about the individual violence of cops on patrol but also the racism that structures the role and purpose of police. This view of racism does not focus on a pathology of an individual person but, rather, on a logic that structures all of society. Structural racism is a logic in which society exists along a hierarchy of value—a global division of humanity—that sorts, classifies, and assigns value to people. Those at the bottom of this hierarchy have less value and, therefore, provide less social value. Their lives matter less. Their deaths matter less. At the top of this hierarchy we find those who have defined their collective racial identity as European, cis-hetero male, and bourgeois. At the bottom we find the others, the Black, Native, poor, and transgender. The Movement for Black Lives, often known as Black Lives Matter, begins with the premise that this structure of racism places Black lives at the bottom of this hierarchy. All Black life is disposable, all Black people are killable, and, in the end, no Black lives matter. As we've noted throughout this book, Native people have similar experiences with racism, which places Native people at the bottom of the global division of humanity—prehuman and nonhuman, in fact, stuck in a state of pre-civilizational primitivity and savagery—and, therefore, also disposable and killable.

Police establish and reproduce racialized social relations and conditions. Police is the institution that quite literally carries out racism on behalf of the state in everyday life. It is, after all, the job of police to fabricate and sustain what they call "law and order," which, in the case of the United States, is an order based on structural racism. This is precisely why BLM protestors have called for the abolition of police as a key step toward the abolition of racism at a structural level. The racism inherent to institutions of the state (the institution of armed police is just one of many) means that Black, Native, and other communities of color are more likely to be subjected to police violence in their everyday lives. Racism in superficially nonviolent state institutions like the law, public education, public transportation, public health, and public housing may not appear "violent," but these institutions establish and reproduce material inequalities that lead to glaring disparities in health and quality of life for Black, Native, and other communities of color. Citizen- and politician-led institutions that claim equity and equality as their goals produce outcomes that reinforce racism that are consistent with the practices of police. This is how structural violence works. It can come in the form of armed police or housing policies that place poor communities of color in polluted neighborhoods or on reservations to make way for white settlement or highways that cut down on white-collar commutes. The result is the same: social and material arrangements that put certain groups in harm's way simply because their lives don't matter according to the logic of racism.

Capitalism exploits more efficiently when paired with racist institutions and ideologies. Racism has allowed capitalism to designate certain populations as exploitable and expendable in the name of economic progress; the onward march of civilization and democracy (a hallmark of liberal societies) that liberal nation-states like the United States constantly laud. In this sense, the political economy of liberalism is, by its very nature, racist and, therefore, violent. Bordertown economies, which reproduce the liberal capitalist settler order of the United States, are no different. Settler colonialism is premised on the ongoing genocide of

Native people and theft of Native land. Capitalism is premised on the exploitation of Native people (and others) and the wastelanding of Native life and land. Liberalism is premised on structural racism and the designation of certain populations as disposable and killable. This entire system is undeniably violent. This is why we add the word *violence* to the word *bordertown*; you simply cannot talk about bordertowns without talking about structural violence, and vice versa.

CHAPTER FIVE

Counterinsurgency

Criminalization

The criminal, and the condition of criminality more generally, does not exist outside of the legal context that creates it. There is no "criminal" where there is no law-abiding citizen. Some version of this idea can be found in all forms of establishment criminological thinking. There is a common notion elaborated by liberal prison reformers, and even by some who subscribe to a conservative law-and-order ideology, that *no one is born a criminal*. A criminal is made through the privations of poverty (according to liberals) or through the particular pathologies of poor minority families (according to conservatives). But this is a liberal capitalist way of thinking that is essential to the operation of settler colonial societies. The view of the criminal as made not born ignores the central fact of life for Native people in settler society. They are born into a settler society that defines their very presence as a violation of what settler law claims as just and lawful. They are born into their criminality. And if the Native person is born into criminality, the settler is born into law-abiding citizenship. In other words, the condition of being the settler is, by its very nature, to be lawful; and the condition of being Native is, by its very nature, to be in perpetual violation of law.

Native people are incarcerated in the United States at a rate nearly 40 percent higher than the national average. According to the Lakota People's Law Project, Native men are incarcerated at four times the rate of white men, and Native women six times the rate of white women. Native people are more likely to be killed by police, convicted of a federal crime, or sent to prison than any other group. This is how "criminalization" works: the settler state's notion of criminality does not just condition Native citizenship, it conditions the very possibility of Native personhood, in that it *anticipates* the Native it sets out to criminalize. This is visible in the way that law has extended to the settler state the right, even the obligation, to engage in the forced sterilization of poor and Native women. To settler law, a Native woman's capacity to have a child is the legal equivalent of harboring a criminal.

All facets of Native life are criminalized in a settler society, and all institutions of settler life, including police, citizenship, and the law, are structured by the criminalization of Native presence. All notions of criminality, including framing legal restitution for land theft and anti-Indianism as "criminal justice," are just modes in the settler's death drive to eliminate the Native.

Boarding Schools

With the publication of his 2006 book *Children Left Behind: The Dark Legacy of Indian Mission Boarding Schools*, Oglala Lakota author Tim Giago broke the silence about the traumatic legacy of Indian boarding schools.[1] He chronicles how children suffered, endured, and died from all manner of physical, emotional, and sexual abuse in these schools. Between 1869 and the 1960s, an estimated one hundred thousand Native children were removed from their homes and placed in boarding schools operated by the federal government and churches. Of the approximately 357 boarding schools that were established after the Carlisle Industrial School, about one-third were managed by Christian denominations. Many Native people tell stories about their experiences in the schools or of those of relatives who suffered similar treatment. Histories of American exceptionalism sanitize boarding school and mission school experiences, denying that they were, in fact, federal government aided, and sometimes directed, acts of genocide. The victims' stories stand in stark contrast to these histories, because they relate how children were removed, often with coercion and force, from their homes, sent to distant schools, where families could not visit, and subjected to violence, simply for being Native.

The roots of US Indian education are reflected in its architect Captain Richard H. Pratt's slogan "kill the Indian, and save the man." "Kill the Indian, and save the man" was an "experiment" to test white society's belief that Indians could be transformed into humans like whites. Their measure of humanity was civilization, and vice versa. The experiment was based on Pratt's program to reform Cheyenne, Arapaho, Comanche, Caddo, and Kiowa prisoners of war at Fort Marion, in St. Augustine, Florida.[2] In 1879, Pratt founded the Carlisle Industrial School in Pennsylvania. Carlisle was an extension of his Fort Marion experiment. As in many of the boarding schools and mission schools that used the Carlisle model, Native children were subjected to military-style living conditions, with an emphasis on corporal punishment and discipline.

Pratt's Indian education measures were endorsed on March 3, 1891, when Congress authorized the Commissioner of Indian Affairs to require Native children to attend boarding schools. The Indian Office worked with the commissioner to force Indian parents and guardians to send their children to boarding schools by withholding rations, clothing, and other annuities. Native families were also imprisoned for refusing to send their children to boarding schools. In 1895, nineteen Hopi leaders, the Kikmongwi, charged with sedition because they refused to allow their children to be sent to the Keams Canyon Boarding School, were imprisoned on Alcatraz Island in San Francisco. The Hopi men spent a year at Alcatraz.

By the end of the 1970s, most boarding schools had shut down. Today, only a few remain open. Many children never returned home, and their fates have yet to be accounted for by the US government. Those who did return experienced and passed on intergenerational trauma and historical trauma—terms that were created to describe the legacy of boarding schools for descendants who continue to identify with ancestral suffering, a "soul wound" that manifests today in the high rates of poverty, all manners of social ills, and a sense of profound loss in Native families. Although First Nations people in Canada have been able to bring worldwide attention to the harms done to their people through residential schools (the Canadian version of boarding schools), in the United States, efforts to hold the government or Catholic Church accountable for the genocidal practices of boarding schools have been largely unsuccessful.

Some Native nations have successfully repatriated the remains of children who died at boarding schools, and community members and educators continue to raise critical consciousness about this history. On December 19, 2009, President Barack Obama signed the Native American Apology Resolution, apologizing for past "ill-conceived policies toward the Native peoples of this land," an apology that essentially has no teeth and has not changed federal policy toward Native people.

Native organizations like the National Congress of American Indians, the International Indian Treaty Council, the Native American Rights Fund, and the National Native American Boarding School Healing Coalition have turned to the United Nations to demand that the US government "provide a full accounting of the children taken into government custody under the US Indian Boarding School Policy whose fate and whereabouts remain unknown."[3]

Race

Race is a social construct, which is to say that imagined biological or genetic origins of so-called group-based racial differences are claims constructed and elaborated through the organizing and categorizing work of social, state, and scientific institutions. The making of difference by race—often presented not as an economic and political project but as a descriptive and self-evident form of difference visible by phenotype and intelligence—relies for its influence on the notion of racial difference as a natural category.

But there is no science of race. Claims of biological or genetic differences by race rely on forms of pseudoscience, usually eugenics, that define racial groups in hierarchical relation to one another. Eugenics was and remains an influential discourse of racial difference that first took hold in the United States in the early to mid–twentieth century. The racist proponents of eugenics argue that group-based racial differences in intelligence and social fitness offer an objective and unequally distributed fact of human life. Most importantly, eugenics is prescriptive in that these racial differences, unless carefully managed, threaten the body politic. It is the job of the state, therefore, to manage belonging by race, usually understood via the language and legal discourse of citizenship. According to eugenicists, the rights and obligations that citizenship confer should not be distributed equally but, rather, must be allotted by the state according to the limits that race places on individuals. The goal of the racial capitalist state, then, was and is to identify superior and inferior individuals, sorted by race, and then to impose social, economic, and political limits, such as fertility limits, limited property rights, and prison sentences, on those considered "unfit." *Unfit* has historically been a racial category applied to Native people, as well as Black and Hispanic people, and also to poor rural whites and those who suffer from mental illness. There is, therefore, a materiality to race. Race may be a social construct, but racial categories matter. As Ruth Wilson Gilmore explains, "Racism, specifically, is the state-sanctioned or extralegal production and exploitation of group-differentiated vulnerability to premature death."[4]

This vulnerability is created and conditioned by all kinds of official policies and practices, often using intelligence tests, such as IQ tests. Only a eugenicist would claim that something called *intelligence* can be measured and correlated to race. Settlers like to measure everything, but it is patently absurd. The fact that something called *intelligence* remains an object of scientific and public interest to the present day suggests that the logic of eugenics, now often packaged under different names—such as genetics or even liberal multiculturalism, in the sense that racial difference structures the logic of the state—remains a powerful racial ideology in US settler society.

Charity

The concept of *charity* in settler society comes directly from the Bible, specifically the verses pertaining to "The Way of Love" that appear in 1 Corinthians 13:1–13 of the New Testament. The love that is spoken of in the New Testament isn't emotional or romantic love but a love that mimics the love of God. The biblical version of love—which was translated from Greek into Latin and eventually into the English word *charity*—refers to goodwill, tolerance, and lofty moral character.

All forms of modern-day charity are inseparable from the power and influence of Christianity. As many Native people have noted, Christianity was and continues to be one of the pillars of the Doctrine of Discovery, which stated that any land not inhabited by Christians was available to be "discovered," claimed, and exploited by Christian rulers and settled by their followers. The doctrine also declared that the Catholic faith and Christianity should be spread so that "the health of souls be cared for and that barbarous nations be overthrown and brought to the faith itself."[5]

The Doctrine of Discovery became the basis of all European claims in the Americas and, later, the foundation for western expansion in the United States. The idea that Christianity should be weaponized to subjugate barbarous nations (read: Native peoples of the Americas) was incorporated into the legal fabric of the United States from its inception as a nation. And the fact that it was paired with European claims to land means that Christianity assumed a central role in justifying the theft and dispossession of Native land, the genocide of Native people, and the liquidation and removal of Native nations from ancestral lands and territories to make way for the growth of the United States and capitalist interests in the West.

In the specific context of present-day US bordertowns, Christianity and its ethos of charity still uphold and reproduce the genocidal, racist intent of the Doctrine of Discovery. One need only drive by a church-run soup kitchen setting up in the early morning hours in a place like Gallup, New Mexico, to see a familiar scene: so-called vagrants and transients, in the words of police, streaming in from their encampments to get a bite to eat. Those serving them, usually white churchgoers and volunteers, appear clean and well-dressed—upstanding US citizens. Those seeking food are usually required to participate in conversion activities (also known as proselytizing) to receive the "selfless" charity of the church. They sing for their supper by receiving moral uplift from Christ for their failings. In this scene, there are two classes of people: Indians, who represent the barbarous nations, and white Christians, who do the virtuous work of US nationalism by dutifully spreading Christianity and caretaking the souls of dirty savages.

Bordertowns are thick with churches. Dozens of denominations compete for funding and visibility to do "charity work" for Native people. Their sole function is to distribute charity through philanthropy and social uplift and, in return, collect souls. But mostly what they collect is money. Churches and nonprofits rake in millions of dollars to "help" Native people under the auspices of charity, yet leave in place the inequity and suffering of Native people. Instead, these institutions and organizations (and the people who work for and worship at them) make a living off the misery of Native people. Rather than practicing a genuine form of equality and love, which Native concepts of kinship express, these institutions profit socially, economically, and culturally off the permanent subjugation of Native people. So long as these purveyors of charity maintain a monopoly on resources and power in bordertowns, so too will the colonial relationship between Native peoples and the United States remain intact. Their relevance—indeed, their very existence—is premised on the permanence of US occupation of Native lands—a performance of the Doctrine of Discovery that never ends. Anyone who espouses decolonization must, therefore, address the inherent colonialism of charity and denounce the churches and nonprofits that benefit from it.

Civil Rights Report

In the summer of 1974, after the Chokecherry Massacre, Navajo activists organized a summer of protests in Farmington, New Mexico. In response to this brutal murder of three Navajo men, the Coalition for Navajo Liberation organized weekly marches through Farmington on seven successive Sundays, effectively closing down the town. White Farmington residents were incensed when the protests interfered with their businesses and profits. The confrontation escalated when Navajo organizers were denied a parade permit by the city of Farmington. Deciding to proceed with their protest, organizers were met with a posse of white settlers dressed in frontier cavalry uniforms. The armed white militia tried to block the parade, and a riot broke out. Police fired teargas into the crowd, and thirty people were arrested.

Navajo protests of these murders by torture were reflective of an era in which Native people were tired of unending anti-Indianism, which was the very fabric of bordertowns like Farmington. The white teens, for example, received minimal sentences for the murders of the three Navajo men, but Red Power activists and community members continued to demand justice. The protests eventually brought the federal Commission on Civil Rights to Farmington in August 1974. The commission commenced investigations into allegations of discrimination against Native people in towns and cities across the country. These investigations, which included public hearings, were focused on off-reservation spaces in South Dakota, Arizona, and New Mexico. Findings indicated that institutional racism and discrimination existed in these bordertowns. Recommendations offered pathways to address racial injustices. Civil rights hearings in Farmington led to the Farmington Report.[6] The report recommended several reforms in San Juan County, including the redistricting of election districts to allow for Navajo participation and lawsuits against the county hospital for refusing to treat Navajos in its emergency room. The US Equal Opportunity Commission also sued the city for employment discrimination.

In late 2005, thirty years after the Chokecherry Massacre, the Commission on Civil Rights released a report on race relations in Farmington that praised the city, pronouncing that race relations had improved. The report stated that "The climate of tolerance and respect between the two cultures is a marked improvement from the conditions the Committee observed 30 years ago in 1974."[7] Yet, in the years between

1974 and 2005, violence against Native peoples, mostly Navajos, continued unabated. In 2006, Clint John, a Navajo man, was killed by a white police officer in Farmington. The incident prompted the Navajo Nation to establish the Navajo Nation Human Rights Commission (NNHRC). The NNHRC addresses Navajo citizens' complaints of racism and discrimination in bordertowns. The commission also brings the Navajo Nation's concerns to the United Nations. In its first four years, the commission hosted twenty-five public meetings to listen to Navajos give testimony about their treatment and experiences in bordertowns. The commission issued their study, "Assessing Race Relations Between Navajos and Non-Navajos," in 2009.[8] The study revealed that racism and discrimination against Navajo citizens in bordertowns has not ended.

The US Civil Rights Commission has failed to resolve complaints of injustice, racism, and discrimination in bordertowns. This is primarily because the settler state refuses to acknowledge that its very foundation depends on the ongoing elimination of Native peoples and dispossession of Native land. The Civil Rights Commission bends to the liberal fictions of diversity and multiculturalism as its practice—as do almost all forms of civil rights when it comes to Indians. While civil rights as a framework has some use when it comes to bordertown violence, only decolonization will end this injustice.

Gender

The conventional settler definition for the word *gender* describes the characteristics of women and men that are socially constructed, while the word *sex* refers to those that are biologically determined. Settlers imposed a Western notion of gender as a binary—feminine and masculine—on Native societies beginning with the earliest invasion of settlers into Native lands. These constructs transformed Native societies in multiple ways.

As feminist scholars have long pointed out, the gender binary offers one source for settler perspectives on how the Earth and land should be treated. The binary dictates that land is feminine and should be conquered, subjugated, and dominated by men. Accounts from the earliest invaders, including Christians, displayed horror about "queer" Native societies that did not regard the land as an object to be dominated. Alarmed by Native peoples' reverence for Earth and the heavens as living beings with which humans could—and did—have relationships, settlers used violence to disrupt these relationships. Once Native peoples had been militarily defeated and removed to reservations, they were then met with legal and social violence designed to coerce them into conforming with heteronormative sensibilities about what "nations" and "families" should look like.

Today, Native people live with disruptions in what are often deemed "private" and "intimate" spaces of the home, where the binary has been most intensely normalized. Subjected to heteronormative arrangements that prioritize relationships between humans, monogamous sexual relations, heterosexual coupling, biological reproduction, male dominance, and marriage, Native people are discouraged from and, in some cases, criminalized for, expressing fluid relationships with humans and other than humans that fall outside the strict confines of the gender binary. Native feminists have pushed back against this, arguing that gender as a category is constructed differently by their societies. Since their creation, Native societies have maintained connections to Mother Earth in specific places and geographies, recognizing a gender diversity that defies and confounds settler needs to restrict gender to practices that uphold and advance capitalism and settler colonialism. Native creation narratives indicate the presence of gender diversity; that third, fourth, and fifth genders, as well as people who identify outside the normative binary, are valued as members of their families and kinship networks. Creation narratives tell histories about the pivotal role that gender-diverse relatives have always played in maintaining ceremonial knowledge, contributing to strong and loving families and ensuring the survival of their people. Today, across Native nations and communities, Native people who identify as nonbinary seek their former status in their own nations and communities as valued members and relatives.

Hate Crime

The label *hate crime* is typically used to bracket a specific kind of violence motivated by extreme prejudice or bigotry. The US Congress defines a *hate crime* as a "criminal offense against a person or property motivated in whole or in part by an offender's bias against race, religion, disability, ethnic origin or sexual orientation."[9] Labeling an act of violence a hate crime assumes intention based on bias. The underlying logic of hate crimes is that the violence results from the perpetrator's extreme bias or hate. The logic goes: the more hateful a hate criminal is, the more violent they will be.

Many politicians, academics, and cops would have us believe that approaching bordertown violence as hate crimes offers the best way to interpret and confront the extremes of violence. This idea relies on a troubling premise. After all, how do you determine the level or intensity of an individual's hate or bigotry? Do we need to prove someone's bigoted motivations to condemn their violence? This is not to say that Native people are not victims of violence based on hatred or that what the settler state calls hate crimes do not happen in bordertowns. Rather, it is to suggest that while hate crimes legislation might offer the legal means to confront individual, vigilante violence against Native people, it is also a logic that primarily serves to obscure the most common mode of settler violence against Native people—good old-fashioned Indian killing (a synonym for Native elimination). In other words, the settler state's attention to hate crimes diverts our attention from the violence at the heart of the settler state itself. It implies that we want regular crimes, not hate crimes, because regular crimes are not as violent. It implies that if we just hire more Native cops (who are presumed to be less racist toward Natives), then the problem of police violence will go away, except for a few "bad apples."

Make no mistake, what the settler state calls hate crimes are no doubt hyperviolent exercises of power, but so too is settler colonialism. Rather than focusing on the bigotry of one individual (which is required for proving intention), as the settler state asks us to, we should focus our efforts on stopping bordertown violence and the larger source of this violence: settler colonialism. This would mean that our practice of resistance should not be based on case-by-case acts of hate. Hate crimes are one type of settler colonial violence; hate killing is Indian killing, and vice versa. The only effective way to stop Indian killing is to destroy settler colonialism through the force of mass movements, thus, also ending the reach and power of individual vigilantes and their hate crimes. Focusing only on the individual nature of hate crimes, however, does nothing to challenge the larger structure of settler colonialism.

Seeing bordertown violence through the lens of hate crimes also points to racism and discrimination as the primary expression of settler colonial desires for Native elimination. At first glance, this seems to make sense given the extreme violence, discrimination, profiling, and surveillance that Native people experience on a daily basis in bordertowns. However, settler colonialism does not target Native people because of their racial difference. It targets Native people because Indians are citizens of Native nations that have ongoing political and territorial claims and often do not recognize the United States as a legitimate authority on Native lands. As a settler state, the United States is threatened by Native claims to land and political authority for the way these claims challenge the idea that the imperial and colonial consolidation of land is a finished project that has produced the greatest nation the world has ever known: the United States. Instead, Native claims to land and political authority—which are the basis of Native nationalism and sovereignty—remind the United States of its failed project of settler colonialism. Not only have Native people never been eliminated, they continue to exercise political, legal, cultural, and social sovereignty in relation to land and water.

Hate crimes are not unique to bordertowns and hate criminals (by legal definition) do not disproportionately target Native people on the basis of race. Rather, hate crimes are ubiquitous in the larger landscape of oppression that describes race, gender, sexuality, and class in the United States. While these forms of oppression intersect with the logic of elimination at the heart of settler colonialism, settler colonialism cannot and should not be reduced to racism or discrimination, because the violence of settler colonialism has its origins in the elimination of Native connections to land and nationhood. Those who call on hate crimes legislation and activism as the way to interpret and rectify bordertown violence must understand the limits of this framework.

History

In June 2020, Native protestors toppled four colonial monuments in New Mexico over the course of four days. Statues of Spanish conquistadors Don Juan de Oñate and Don Diego de Vargas and of Indian Killer Kit Carson, as well as an obelisk in the city center of Santa Fe celebrating US wars against "savage Indians," all fell in quick succession. The actions fulfilled a dream twenty years in the making and marked the beginning of the newest surge in Native resistance in New Mexico.

The backlash was swift, violent, and racist. Counterprotestors, many who claimed "pure" Spanish blood, took to social media to decry the removals and minimize the genocidal crimes of the conquistadors. Some claimed that the statues of conquistadors represented their cultural heritage as descendants of Spanish colonialism. They deployed familiar anti-Indian tropes: Native women and youth who participated in statue removals were "violent criminals." They called for "bounties" on the heads of anonymous individuals who spray painted phrases like "This Is Tewa Land" on racist monuments in Santa Fe. They declared The Red Nation, one of the groups that organized the toppling of the Oñate statue, among the most controversial of the monuments, as an "anti-Hispanic hate group." A right-wing militia group with documented connections to local police in Albuquerque led the counterprotests.

This response was expected. New Mexico whitewashes its history and its ongoing pattern of anti-Indianism and organized violence against Native peoples through a myth of "tri-cultural harmony" that depicts the violence of conquest as firmly in the past. The myth renders colonialism as a violent but unfortunate history that New Mexico's supposed cultural groups—Hispanos, whites, and Indians—have moved beyond, now coexisting peacefully. This myth absolves settlers of past and present settler colonial violence and underwrites the entire tourist economy of New Mexico. This is big business. Tourism based on this myth draws millions of people and hundreds of millions of dollars to the state every year.

The ideology of "tri-cultural harmony" permeates every aspect of public life in New Mexico, promoting the idea that white, Hispano, and Native groups are on equal footing. This imaginary equality comes from the so-called shared "cultural" contributions of each group, the sum of which is said to create the unique history of "cultural exchange" in New Mexico that draw tourists and their dollars. The myth folds differences or conflicts between these groups into the category of "culture" (or a "clash of cultures," a common trope in Southwest historiography). The myth elevates "harmony" as a kind of default mode in New Mexico. The myth works to minimize conflict between or among groups as merely disharmony that requires "cultural sensitivity" toward others by those blamed for creating disharmony.

Many of the outraged Hispano supporters of conquistador statues relied on this myth to argue that social change cannot come from "riots"— their term for Native protests that forced local governments to remove the statues. No, change only comes from fostering "respect" between different cultures, they argued. This logic was the logic of the Democratic mayor of Santa Fe when he called for the establishment of a truth and reconciliation commission following the removal of Don Diego de Vargas and Kit Carson statues in the city. In other words, the problem is not structural racism, histories of genocide, or ongoing settler colonial vigilante and police violence. The problem is only about a few individuals and a few bad acts. And, therefore, the solution cannot be the return of stolen lands or the observance of treaty obligations. Instead, the solution is found in cultural understanding defined by liberal notions of peace and healing.

The premise of nearly all establishment histories of New Mexico relies on the myth of tri-cultural harmony. From this premise come familiar conclusions that Native history is important only insofar as it makes a "cultural" contribution to the greater good of the "American melting pot." The phrase came into existence in the mid-1990s during the height of multiculturalism in the United States. The notion of American multiculturalism rose to prominence following the 1992 quincentenary of Columbus's supposed discovery of America. The idea gained traction for the way it offered sanitized and instrumental versions of New Mexico's settler colonial past.

The histories that rely on this myth spin tales of a common heritage shared by Native peoples and other groups by virtue of the blended cultures (a euphemism for bordertown violence) and intermarriage (a euphemism for rape and slavery) that shaped present-day New Mexico. "I'm not racist, I'm married to a Native American" or "I'm not racist, I have the blood of the conqueror and of the conquered coursing through my veins" are familiar refrains that settlers often use to avoid the accusations of anti-Indian racism against those who support statues of Oñate in Ohkay Owingeh and Albuquerque.

You will find this culture industry everywhere in New Mexico: public museums, festivals, art markets, architecture, murals, cathedrals, and truth and reconciliation commissions. In the context of ongoing colonial dispossession, culture operates as a scam to aid and abet colonial plunder. New Mexico consistently records among the highest number of police killings each year—and ranks last in education and health care for Native people. New Mexico transformed itself into an oil and gas powerhouse, largely by fracking on and adjacent to Navajo and Pueblo lands, an industry that has brought man camps, rape, and pollution to tribal communities over the past fifteen years. Meanwhile, the lesson history teaches us is harmony, so Native people should accept subjugation. Don't protect your heritage, sell it and live in harmony with your colonizers. Colonialism is in the past. This is the present; get over it.

Liberal multiculturalism converts Native claims to land into a racial category. In other words, it's not about land, it's about culture. You won't get the land back, history promises, but you could make some money on your culture. This is conquest with a new face. Native people must self-regulate and self-discipline as good Indians to sustain the exchange value of their culture. When they refuse their subjugation by blockading resource extraction routes into tribal lands or protesting celebrations of conquest, they abandon this carefully delimited category of identity. These are bad Indians and must be blamed and hated for disrupting the cultural harmony settlers brought to New Mexico. They must be condemned and swiftly punished by the public and by the police. Their histories do not matter outside histories of settler colonialism that portray the present as a profound accomplishment. The present is progress, and, thus, Native activism against the present—whether by the toppling of statues or the blockading of pipelines—represents a crime against the past and violations against the sanctity of culture.

Bad Indians don't get museums and festivals and doctorates to tell histories of resistance and suffering. Anytime they tell these histories, settler historians pummel them with objectivity, that Bible of settler history. "There are always two sides to every story," historians remind them. These historians love to talk about a "balanced history" and "the meeting of cultures." Native histories that refuse these criteria are not history, they are too presentist, too activist, or too political—settler code words for biased—and summarily dismissed. This, of course, never works the other way around, as the magnanimous and triumphal narrative of tri-cultural harmony demonstrates.

If history seeks truth, as we are taught, then US history offers no truth. Objectivity is a scam. And tri-cultural harmony is a ploy designed to prevent us from seeing settler colonialism for what it really is. Tie a chain around it, pull it to the ground, dump it in the river.

CHAPTER SIX

Settler Scams

Property

All claims to private property are stories about beginnings. Like all good fiction, the story that settlers tell of private property includes four elements. There are characters in the story of their property. There is a scene that the settler must set. Their claims unfold like a plot. And all of this inexorably leads to an ending. All stories must come to an end.

Let's start with characters. There are always so many characters in the story of settler property. The hero, of course, is the settler. And the story is populated by throngs of settler hangers-on—cowboys, Indian agents, railroad barons, trappers, and traders. The Indian, however, rarely gets a part. When elites among Spanish settlers first claimed land in what is now Mexico and the United States, for example, they wrote petitions for land, usually to colonial bureaucrats. In these petitions they spun tales about unused and uninhabited lands. The Indian, in other words, has no role in the story of settler property. The only character available for the reader to root for is our settler, who heroically tames wild lands and brings civilization to the frontier

These wild lands on the frontier describe the scene of settler property. Scene-setting is crucial for all stories, but perhaps none more so than the stories of settler private property. Scene-setting is a challenge, because, on the one hand, the setting must be specific. It must describe a specific territory or tract of land. But, on the other hand, the reader expects an epic. It must happen everywhere. Private property must be universal. How does one write a story that takes in all the world? Simple. This is the specialty of the settler. All settler stories are stories of settler possession. Our hero, the Christian, white, male, head of household, etc., must, in fact, be a hero, which means he must vanquish a foe. This poses a problem, because the obvious foe would be an Indian, but the Indian cannot appear in the story as a fully formed human character. To do so would risk establishing the Indian as the underdog. The settler cannot risk losing the reader's loyalty from the hero to the Indian. That would be almost as bad as losing land, so the settler takes this problem seriously. Settler scene-setting requires some creativity. So the settlers established special schools that they call law schools. At those schools, they developed three scene-setting solutions to the "hero" problem.

The first solution to this problem is to ignore the Indian entirely by depicting all the world as a settler world. Pretend the Indian just doesn't exist. Write them out of the scene. A lot of "the greats" chose this option—John Muir, Henry David Thoreau, Abraham Lincoln. A second option includes Indians as characters, but only as savages preying on white women. By vanquishing the savage Indian, the white male settler becomes a hero and, thus, worthy of property. This is a common and effective choice, because it locates property's origins in settler colonialism and masculinity. Andrew Jackson comes to mind. A third option requires the most finesse, and only the most skillful settler chooses it. In this version, the author of settler property admits Indians into the scene as characters, but only as noble savages. The Indian is not the settler's foe in this story. No, in fact, the Indian and the settler are friends. The hero is sympathetic and attuned to the plight of the vanishing Indian. The author reveals the "plight" of the Indian through contrast. The settler hero is industrious, the Indian lazy. The settler embodies progress, the Indian backwardness. The settler holds his liquor, the Indian cannot. This is the paternalistic version of settler property that Supreme Court Justice John Marshall perfected. This third option often included a bonus. If the Indian is not the foe, who will the settler vanquish to become a hero? The answer: Mexicans. The hero defeats the Mexicans and saves the Indian. The Indian is then invited to tour America under armed guard and give many speeches far from their homelands, where settlers were busy building a bordertown on a former Native village. This option is appealing, because it establishes a US settler claim to Native land and to Mexico.

Scene-setting establishes the settler's specific private property claim. The plot to this story is often an afterthought. These are not very interesting or believable stories, in other words. Plots require details, which are the enemies of settler property claims.

This brings us to the end, but there is no end to the story of settler private property. There is no ending, because there can be no ending, at least not on the settler's terms. And the settler knows this, which is why the settler pretends that settler private property isn't a story at all. Rather, it is law, they tell us. Or it is nature. Or it is progress. But we know it is none of these things. Property is a made-up story that the settler tells about their world, and a lousy one at that. A fiction on top of a fiction. Nothing more.

Nonprofit

The 1969 Tax Reform Act created Section 501(c)3 of the United States Internal Revenue Service Code. The section provides for organizations to claim a tax-exempt status as private foundations and charities. The law created the basis for a new type of organization: the nonprofit. By 1980, the nonprofit sector had grown so large that it was considered a third sector on par with government and business. This was not just true in the United States. The creation of this third sector was intentional. The origins of this new tax-exempt status can be found in corporate boardrooms not on the streets. In 1973, the Filer Commission, a group of ruling-class politicians and CEOs brought together by the Rockefeller family, issued a report that called for this third sector—a sector of private funding and support for humanitarian and philanthropic organizations. The commission wished for this third sector to play an important role in American life and politics.

The era of the tax-exempt nonprofit emerged on the heels of some of the largest social movements in US history. Along with groups engaged in popular and widespread resistance against the Vietnam War, liberation formations like civil rights, women's liberation, and Red Power transformed public consciousness around long-ignored issues of social, racial, environmental, and economic justice. Many individual groups started or joined tax-exempt nonprofit organizations, which many believed provide funding streams in support of the long-term institutional and societal changes these groups sought. But nonprofits quickly absorbed the revolutionary energy of this era. Instead of fostering a revolutionary social transformation, the sector created a new class of workers: the cultural and social entrepreneur. These so-called "changemakers," as they thought of themselves, sought to design programs for progressive causes by raising money from wealthy donors like the corporations that founded the 1973 Filer Commission. Nonprofits quickly became lucrative operations, turning revolution into charity and movements into million-dollar foundations.

From its origins in the Filer Commission, the nonprofit has always been a key way for ruling-class elites to muzzle, placate, or seek to control the revolutionary elements of the 1960s and 1970s, movements that sought class abolition and an end to capitalism not a better tax status for wealthy philanthropists. Through changes in the US tax code, corporate executives sought to buy off these movements with the promise of consistent charitable donations. In other words, nonprofits transformed social and political struggle into a tax-exempt industry, defanging revolutionary movements in ways that preserved the relations and conditions of production for capitalists to continue accumulating wealth and power uninterrupted. The emergence of the nonprofit sector (what many aptly call an industrial complex) has been one of the hallmarks of neoliberalism.

The nonprofit sector dominates every corner of Indian Country today, raising money to end Native misery by treating Native people as charitable causes. Vine Deloria famously joked in his 1969 polemic *Custer Died for Your Sins: An Indian Manifesto* that Indians suffer from the proliferation of government and nonprofit programs designed to help the seemingly pitiful and needy Indian.[1] Bordertowns also suffer from this disease (what some jokingly call "programitis"), with Native people constantly treated like charity cases by churches, health care institutions, local governments, and even cops—wretches unable to care for themselves and their relatives and in desperate need of private and governmental welfare.

The nonprofit sector has not delivered Native liberation to Indian Country—it has no interest in doing so—and, therefore, Native people should pause before they leap to create one. Why is our first impulse for enacting change the establishment of a nonprofit? Who will these nonprofits serve? We should understand the history of the nonprofit within its neoliberal context and ask why and how we have been convinced to think nonprofits are the best (or only) way to promote change for our communities. What should we expect out of a sector that funnels our energies into—and ensures our perpetual dependence on—financial systems controlled by the ruling class?

When we build and sustain nonprofits, we sustain and reinforce the authority of settler society's ruling class over us. They will give us some money, but only if we soften our demands for an end to the exploitation of

Native life. They do not support Native liberation but, rather, throw a few pennies at us to create more programs to alleviate our "condition." And they do this to sustain an existing settler order, one structured around the theft of our future and the destruction of our lands. The nonprofit sector smuggles capitalist ideology into our communities through the language of philanthropy and the pathologizing of Native people as charity cases. Anti-capitalist organizing is our only legitimate alternative and the only one capable of leading us to a Native future on this planet.

Sacred Sites

"Defend the sacred!" is a political slogan seen on rally signs and heard in protest chants in bordertowns where Native people and environmentalists advocate for the protection of landscapes and waterways from environmental degradation. A popular banner created for the #NODAPL uprising at Standing Rock depicts a striking image of Asdzáá Tl'ogi (Weaver Woman), one of the wives of famed Navajo Chief Manuelito, alongside the phrase *defend the sacred*, in capital letters. Photos of the banner from Standing Rock quickly went viral. The image of hundreds gathered behind the banner, marching toward the front lines, galvanized international support for this uprising. The #NODAPL struggle sought to stop the oil flowing through the Dakota Access Pipeline, which threatened the Missouri River, a waterway that many who became known as water protectors claimed as sacred to the Lakota and Dakota people. This slogan and the accompanying image of a powerful Native woman imply that "Mother Earth"—a concept and phrase often used to describe Native concepts of *the environment*—is under attack by capitalism. Our duty is to protect and defend our planetary mother from threats that would seek to desecrate her life-giving force.

It is considered common knowledge that the life-giving force of Mother Earth is one that sustains all life on this planet. Environmentalists often attribute this discourse to Native philosophies and spiritual rituals that are said to center reverence for the environment. The idea of a sacred site comes from this discourse. The logic goes as follows: Mother Earth gives us all life. The capacity to give life is sacred. Capital-driven industrial pollution violates this sacredness. Our collective practice of resistance must defend and protect Mother Earth so she can continue to give life and so Native people can continue to practice their religious and spiritual traditions in concert with Mother Earth.

It is true that for many Native people Earth is sacred, because she is the mother of all life. But it is important to be critical about how the term *sacred* is taken up within politics. The discourse of the sacred is gendered. As the image of Asdzáá Tł'ógi implies, Mother Earth is a woman. Like Mother Earth, women are considered sacred because of their capacity to give life through the process of biological reproduction (childbirth). Thus, any violation of Native women is seen as a violation of Mother Earth and the land, and vice versa. This is why the phrase *rape of Mother Earth* has become a popular rejoinder in environmentalist and feminist ideas about Native resistance. The term *rape* is typically reserved for the violation of women. Because both women and the Earth share in the sacredness inherent to the capacity to give life, "rape" applies equally to both.

Definitions of the sacred that are attached to childbirth limit concepts of *gender*. They presume that biological womanhood (or manhood, for that matter) defines Native peoples and their politics of resistance. This is called gender essentialism by queer feminists. Kim TallBear argues that we should not presume a natural link between political resistance to capitalism and the biological imperative of reproduction that privileges cis-hetero Native women. The discourse of the sacred relies on the idea that biological reproduction is the basis of gender. This is why advocates of sacred sites portray Mother Earth as a cis-hetero Native woman. This definition of gender excludes LGBTQI2S relatives who do not perform— and, in some cases, refuse—these limited gender expectations based on biological definitions of caretaking and life. LGTBQI2S politics are at the center of Native resistance to bordertown violence. Because of its gender essentialism, the discourse of the sacred as it currently stands cannot advance the LGBTQI2S struggle. It may, therefore, be inappropriate as a basis for Native resistance to bordertown violence.

Peace and Healing

What does it mean to take up *peace* and *healing* as part of the struggle for Native liberation? How might we revise our understanding of peace and healing to imagine a world that prioritizes collective well-being and healthy relationships? The starting point is to reclaim these terms from the neoliberal realm of trauma and nonprofit program that strips them of their revolutionary potential.

Indian experts have spent the last forty years fundraising and developing programs to address trauma. These experts have created terms like *intergenerational trauma*, *historical trauma*, and *genetic trauma* to describe the horrific impact of colonialism on Native (and Black) life. *Trauma* has become a keyword in everyday Native life to describe the spectrum of harm and abuse experienced living under colonial occupation. This means Native people are keenly aware that trauma comes from colonialism. Trauma undoubtedly describes the everyday landscapes of exploitation and discrimination that characterize Native life in bordertowns.

Trauma, like colonialism, is undeniably real, and if we ignore it, we ignore the needs of Native people. The treatment of trauma in Native communities is necessary and requires specialists who are trained in trauma-informed care to help individuals and families heal.

However, as Athabascan feminist Dian Million has pointed out, under neoliberalism trauma expanded into a full-blown paradigm, becoming a paradigmatic therapeutic politics.[2] The term *historical trauma* is one of the most prevalent examples of therapeutic politics, referring to a structural phenomenon that transcends time and space; a continuum of harm that colonialism perpetrates across generations, to the point where it is embedded in Native peoples' DNA. Another key example of therapeutic politics is the era of reconciliation that Canada implemented in the early 2000s as part of the Indian Residential Schools Settlement Agreement. Native scholars have heavily criticized reconciliation, underscoring how the therapeutic language of trauma and healing that informs reconciliation does very little to redress Native claims for justice, which at minimum require mass land return and the total abolition of Canadian settler colonialism. Instead, what Native people have been offered by Canada is more inclusion in the halls of power and more money for social programs. This sounds very similar to the invention and purpose of nonprofits (another hallmark of neoliberalism), which was to quell radical political demands coming out of the revolutionary period of the 1960s and 1970s by turning outrage at Native suffering—trauma—into a charitable enterprise. And while Canada touts reconciliation as an era of so-called peace between First Nations and the Canadian settler state, Native people continue to experience high rates of violence. The state crackdown in February 2020 on Unist'ot'en Camp in unceded Wet'suwet'en territory is one glaring example of this. Peace means nothing without justice, and justice requires land return and the end of settler colonialism.

We have already seen what happens when trauma becomes the basis for righting the wrongs of colonialism. Reconciliation uses the language of trauma to neutralize Native demands for decolonization. Although less insidious, historical trauma individualizes and personalizes colonialism, focusing on its victims rather than dismantling colonialism itself. Within these projects, peacemaking and healing become another avenue—a trick—of settler societies to defer Native liberation. Meanwhile, the real causes of trauma—colonialism and capitalism—remain intact.

And as trauma and healing have become more prominent within Native politics and institutions, space for other strategies and visions of change shrink. Trauma now consumes the majority of our political energy. This narrowing of our politics has come at the expense of building vibrant and militant struggles for liberation with other colonized and oppressed peoples of the world. Movements outside the United States and Canada rarely traffic in the language of trauma and healing to develop political positions on decolonization and liberation. In this time of global pandemic, we must reclaim peace and healing from the First World (neoliberal) paradigm of trauma and instead globalize our efforts to liberate the planet from systems and structures that target whole nations and species. Although there are many points of entry into this global struggle, there can be no doubt that Native movements for decolonization and liberation must be at the center of our collective efforts.

Police Brutality

The phrase *police brutality* is commonly used by police reformers, whether liberal or conservative, to describe police violence that is considered "excessive." It is reformist, rather than transformational, because it seeks to preserve the institution that engages in the violence: police. In other words, while the phrase suggests that police inflict "illegal" or "extralegal" violence, it relies on an understanding of police as something other than an institution that manages and specializes in violence. To talk about the problem of police, policing, and police violence as a problem of "police brutality" is to talk about police the way cops talk about police. Consider the grammar of the phrase. The word *brutality* modifies the word *police*, which suggests that the police institution is not sufficiently descriptive enough. In other words, without *brutality*, *police* is just *police*. Therefore, the story *police brutality* tells about police is one in which police is always potentially good and just. The phrase leaves open the possibility that police serve an objective common good that has somehow gone awry but can be fixed through reformist interventions, such as hiring more Native cops, improving training, and raising hiring standards. To call for an end of police brutality, therefore, is not to call for an end to police violence; rather, it is to call for more "justified" police violence.

What is "justified" police violence? The word *justified* in the context of police advances an essential cop premise: the idea that civilization is a cop accomplishment achieved through the application of legitimate violence. Understanding this is important in any consideration of border-town violence, because the opposite of civilization, in the police lexicon, is savagery. The proper subject of police, and, thus, of police violence, is often depicted as the "savage." Police, we are told, bring security and order, and this requires the subjugation of the savage.

The civilization/savagery binary structures anti-Indian common sense more generally. From its origins, America represented itself as that which stood opposed to the Native. Thomas Jefferson imagined America as itself a war against "merciless Indian savages." At the heart of anti-Indian common sense, therefore, is the idea that the savage cannot be managed, it must be eliminated. As Phil Deloria explains, "many Americans came to view [Indians] as savages who, if they refused to disappear, deserved extermination."[3] What is extermination if not genocide? And what is the police, that institution charged with inaugurating civilization, if not an agency of genocide? And what is *police brutality* if not a phrase designed to obfuscate all this?

Human Rights

Human rights is a concept central to the constitution and function of the liberal settler state. If you want rights, you need the state, which presents itself always as the origin and guarantor of human rights. Let's first dispense with the idea that *human rights* has anything whatsoever to do with anything we might consider intrinsic to the human condition. It is not a concept that exists independent of the settler state. There is no ahistorical, objective notion of belonging animated by the state. There is no shared language and practice of care constructed by the state. There is no intrinsically just and moral expression of "being in the world" discovered, brought to life, and defended by the state.

Human rights is an ideological concept that solves two vexing problems for the settler state. First, it reserves for the state the right to limit belonging. If you are not a citizen, your rights are another's concern. In this way, the settler state becomes merely the caretaker of some imaginary, preexisting, inalienable human right, a seemingly objective category behind which the settler state hides its ruthlessness.

Second, *human rights* tell private property's origin story. If you are a subject of a settler state, you may claim certain "human rights," and they will be theoretically guaranteed by the state, but they will not provide an actual means for your survival beyond market exchange. "Human rights" are defined as rights between and among people that are guaranteed and preserved by the state. Land has nothing to do with it. If *human rights* were a concept organized around relations to land, there would be no settler state. Thus, the liberal settler state relies on the concept of *human rights* to define justice and belonging through private property. You have the right to be exploited via the wage relation—and nothing more.

Native peoples find state-based "human rights" to be an incoherent concept, which explains why Native activists and organizers pursued claims to Native rights beyond the nation-state. Consider the United Nations Declaration on the Rights of Indigenous Peoples (UNDRIP), which defines Native freedom as a condition based in land and collective in nature. Unlike settler notions of *human rights* purposefully abstracted from the material conditions of living, UNDRIP identifies a specific threat to Native rights (settler colonialism) and identifies specific conditions without which Native peoples cannot be free. Native peoples have the right to be free from the "forced assimilation or destruction of their culture," the right to be free from the colonial dispossession "of their lands, territories or resources," the right to be free from settler states "forcibly removing children," and the right to be free from being "forcibly removed from their lands or territories."

UNDRIP was adopted by the United Nations General Assembly on September 13, 2007. Nearly 150 states around the world endorsed the declaration. The United States, Canada, Australia, and New Zealand, however, refused to sign. This was not a surprise. The Declaration is a document of decolonization. Its intended audience is not the Native peoples who wrote it but the settler states that refused to sign it. Consider the implication. All of the conditions from which Native peoples must be free are also all of the conditions that make the United States, Canada, Australia, and New Zealand possible. These are states based on the theft of Native land and the destruction of Native kinship. Their futures depend on their ability to sustain this. This is why we define settler states as political entities of Native unfreedom arbitrated through the mechanism of human rights.

Liberalism

"Life, liberty, and the pursuit of happiness." This phrase is famous. It is synonymous with *America*. This phrase likely adorned the wall of your kindergarten, where most first learned that America stands for these values, and that because of these values this country represents the most unique and special political system in world history. We find the phrase in the Declaration of Independence. Thomas Jefferson, one of the founding fathers of America, borrowed the phrase from a British philosopher named John Locke—one of the founding fathers of liberalism—who penned a slightly different version of the phrase, "life, liberty, and property," in a book called *Two Treatises of Government*, which was published in 1689 and is one of the most important books in the history of liberal thought.[4]

When we speak of liberalism, we don't mean *liberals* in its common usage to describe people with left-of-center politics. A liberal is someone who stands for life, liberty, and the pursuit of happiness. This can and does include most Americans, Canadians, and Europeans, regardless of where they sit on the political spectrum. But what does it mean to pursue life, liberty, and happiness? For Locke, life, liberty, and estate are best secured through ownership and dominion over property. The history of the United States is a history of the mass conversion of life into property. This has included (and continues to include) land, human beings, cells, animals, water, air, time, aquifers, oil, rock, and more. Liberals turn pretty much anything into property if it can turn a profit.

Liberals insist that democracy, liberty, and equality are ideal forms of political organization. Phrases like "America is the greatest country on Earth" and the job of the United States is to "spread democracy throughout the globe" offer common versions of this exceptionalism. Note that these phrases make no mention of the role of property. In a liberal society, property is the basis for creating and accumulating wealth and power. Here's a common scenario in the United States: if you are financially able to buy a home, you are said to be a property owner. If you fix up your property, you can sell it for a profit. You can then use that profit to acquire more property, whether it be a nicer house or a nicer car, or you can invest that money in stocks, bonds, or other property to make even more profit. Members of wealthier classes do this on a grander scale with resources like oil and steel or, in the case of health care, treatments or procedures that can be patented, which requires the conversion of knowledge into property. Regardless of the scale, property ownership begets greater wealth in a liberal society, and we are constantly told that owning property—and passing it down to our progeny—should be our greatest goal in life.

History shows us that liberalism has always been paired with incredible wealth and power precisely because property plays such an essential role in creating liberal ideology. How did nations like England, France, or the United States build the wealth they're now known for? For England and France, this happened through the conquest of much of Africa and Asia and subsequent possession of vast swaths of territory, peoples, and resources by these imperial nations. For the United States, this happened through the genocide of Native peoples, theft and privatization of Native land, enslavement and possession of Black Africans, and exploitation of migrant labor. These imperial and colonial practices of possession birthed liberalism by turning diverse forms of life into property that could be possessed, exploited, and traded for profit and power. Therefore, we can't unmoor equality or democracy or freedom from the violence of property relations if we wish to understand liberalism.

So what does this have to do with bordertown violence? Bordertowns are settlements that lie within the jurisdiction of the United States; they are claimed by the United States as American towns and cities. Thus, they carry out the project of American liberalism. To be patriotic in America is to love the liberal values this nation is built upon. "Most Patriotic Small Town in America," the slogan of the notorious bordertown of Gallup, New Mexico, is an obvious example of this. But to be patriotic also means you uphold the violence of property relations that makes liberalism tick. Native people in bordertowns—especially the poor and unsheltered—have a strong understanding of how liberalism works because of the way they are criminalized and policed to protect the sanctity of private property. Anti-panhandling laws and everyday policing in bordertowns protect businesses, gated homes, and infrastructure instead of Native life. In fact, Native people are seen as a threat to the sanctity of private property, despite being in their own homelands. This manifests primarily as Indian killing in bordertowns, which is a social, legal, and physical mechanism for carrying out the liberal settler project of Native genocide and land theft. The United States claims to bring liberalism to the rest of the "uncivilized" world, including Indian Country, through democracy. If Native people reject these so-called gifts of democracy, we are deemed hostile, a threat to democracy, property, and liberty that must be eliminated. This is how liberalism works in bordertowns: to civilize and manage us or, if we don't conform, eliminate us.

Tourism

You can rent a tipi for the night in Montana or spend a weekend in a hogan in New Mexico. You can take "Indian tours" on reservations throughout North America. You can carve a birch bark canoe in Maine or a totem pole in British Columbia. What's on offer in all of these cases is an "authentic" tourist experience, an opportunity to "play Indian." "Our customers want to understand Native America," explained one tour guide, "rather than a made-up culture." According to the Dakota scholar Vine Deloria, it is through tourism that non-Indian people come to believe they know Native people. "Understanding Indians is not an esoteric art," he writes. "All it takes is a trip through Arizona or New Mexico. . . . Mention Indians and you will find a person who saw some in a gas station in Utah, or who attended the Gallup ceremonial celebration. . . . There is no subject on earth so easily understood as that of the American Indian."[5]

Deloria's brilliant satire reveals a common thread consistent to all forms of tourist knowledge of Natives, whether in claims by Christian missionaries, station wagons full of vacationers, or anthropologists "studying" Native people. Each of these examples share a common claim to the "easy knowledge" acquired via a tourist-based exchange relation. It might be true that, nominally, the tourist buys a blanket or a bracelet or the missionary collects a soul or the anthropologist gets a job as an Indian expert, but in all cases the thing they're really after is "knowledge of Indians"—this is the commodity of tourism—and the perceived authority over Natives that the sale of this commodity confers to the tourist. In other words, the exchange value of a woven blanket or turquoise necklace or a night spent in a Tipi is based on the use value of that particular commodity. According to Karl Marx, a thing has use value—a term he uses to refer to the specific utility of a particular object or thing—only because of the abstract human labor objectified or materialized in it. In other words, the tourist wants that Indian blanket, because it offers itself as the material objectification of Native knowledge. This is what the tourist is after. It is this that the tourist must possess and ultimately claim authority over.

Most importantly, use value represents the abstract human labor congealed in the commodity. This is to say that the Native people who actually make the jewelry or rent the hogans or lead the tours matter to the tourist only as a category—the Indian—and only insofar as it can be interpreted by the tourist.

Tradition

There are many definitions of Native tradition. When Native people talk about tradition, they do not always define it (or use it) the same way. Native feminists have pointed out that tribal politicians often select specific ideas about Native tradition to justify the dominance of cis-hetero men in tribal leadership. These uses of tradition reinforce Christian settler ideals about gender and sexuality that keep straight Native men in power and Native women and LGBTQI2S relatives in subservient positions. They also bolster ideologies of tribal nationalism that discriminate against tribal citizens who do not conform to gender binaries (man/woman) and apologize for perverse gender and sexual violence that can be absolved through ceremony.

Native activists use Native tradition in other ways. It is common to hear talk about cultural revitalization, reclamation, and resurgence (the three R's) in activist circles. Activists who attach their ideas about decolonization to the three R's typically look to Native traditions like ceremonies and philosophies for frameworks of justice and historical transformation. How activists employ Native traditions within these frameworks, however, is diverse. Some consolidate traditional Native religious practices into the concept of *the sacred* to bolster environmental justice claims. Others claim that conservation—which often comes in the form of green capitalism—is a traditional Native ethic that emerges from the perceived closeness of Native people to nature. Still others are captivated by the optic of historical trauma to explain the violence of colonization. The solution these activists propose is a process of healing from trauma—both individual and collective—that draws on versions of Native tradition that vary from New Age interpretations of sweat lodging and drumming to highly specialized and tribally specific ceremonial practices. Advocates of trauma-based interpretations of Native tradition view healing as a radical (and perhaps paramount) act of decolonization.

Within academic spaces Native tradition is used as a model for education. The idea that Indians think in circles is one of the most popular examples of this usage, often accompanied by images of medicine wheels and four-directional flowcharts. Movements to "indigenize" or "decolonize" curriculum and academic knowledge often draw on select concepts of traditional Native knowledge to replace or critique Western epistemologies. The model of Sa'ah Naghai Bik'en Hozho is one such conceptual framework that has been popularized within Navajo education as a "Diné methodology" distinct from Western methodology.

Almost all of these approaches cast tradition as transcendent. The Oxford English Dictionary defines tradition as "the transmission of customs or beliefs from generation to generation" or "a doctrine believed to have divine authority."[6] This definition points to the fundamental consistency of tradition across time and space, one that we should revere and not question. This is why most invocations of tradition are prescriptive and conservative, implying a "return" to something sacrosanct and unchanged.

Because of its perceived transcendence, any questioning of Native tradition is treated as an act of desecration bordering on profanity. For this reason, critiques of tradition are heavily policed within Native activist communities, families, public discourse, and spheres of governance. We should be wary of those who claim they have a purer interpretation of Native tradition. These advocates may just be reinforcing a form of social conservatism that refuses to acknowledge that politics arise from specific histories, social relations, and political contexts. Certainly, there are aspects of tradition that ought to revered and respected. There are likewise positive and revolutionary methods to be found in Native traditions. But to presume that Native tradition exists outside of history is a dangerous proposition that obscures the ways tradition is put to work for violent ideologies and political projects like heteropatriarchy, liberalism, and capitalism. These ideologies and projects seek to conserve—not change—existing orders. Tradition is not transcendent, it is selective. There are many forms of tradition that do not align with the goals of Native liberation. In fact, they obstruct these goals. Instead of naturalizing the transcendence of tradition, our deployment of tradition should bolster specific political ideologies and goals that facilitate Native liberation.

CHAPTER SEVEN

Burn the Village

Abolition

Slavery, imprisonment, and punishment were the earliest forms of class war. It is no accident, then, that mass incarceration is a defining feature of settler colonialism today or that the abolition of the prison and its camp guards, the police, is central to decolonization. In fact, African abolition and Native liberation movements have been tethered together since the very beginning of colonization.

The plantation was the first bordertown, the first settlement that trespassed into Native land. The plantation paved the way for later English settlements, most famously Plymouth Plantation. In 1526, Lucas Vázquez de Ayllón, a Spanish slaver, founded North America's first European colonial settlement, San Miguel de Guadalupe, in what is currently South Carolina. With him, Ayllón brought a hundred enslaved Africans and Native Caribbeans and hundreds of Spanish settlers. A year later, the enslaved Africans joined their Native brethren to overthrow the Spanish colonizers. It was the first successful slave revolt in the Americas. Once the Europeans left, the self-emancipated Africans lived among the Guales, the Native peoples of the land, becoming the first non-Native peoples to live permanently in North America. These communities formed not by dispossessing, displacing, or eliminating Native peoples, but by joining together in anti-colonial solidarity.

For three centuries, European slavers pillaged the African continent, stealing human beings. These manhunters kidnapped, shackled, and chained more than twelve million Africans, transforming them into merchandise to be bought and sold alongside other goods and services in the so-called "New World." Millions perished during the perilous transatlantic voyage—and some dove from the slave ships into the dark waters, choosing the freedom of death over a life of bondage. Slave traders stripped babies from mothers, severing African kinship relations with land and family in a cruel calculation for profit.

The most valuable asset of kidnapped Africans was their labor time—their capacity to work. At the end of a whip, their descendants picked the cotton and harvested the crops creating the capital that fueled US westward expansion. Stolen Native lands were required to reap profit from generation after generation of stolen African labor. The plantation system was the economic engine that powered US settler colonialism, and it was shackled African hands and muscles that built the first nation born entirely as a capitalist state.

But the African people were more than cargo. With them, they brought their own cultures and traditions, their own ways of knowing and being in relation with the world, giving rise to one of the most potent revolutionary traditions in world history, the Black Radical Tradition, first premised on the utter annihilation and abolition of the system of racial capitalism embodied in chattel slavery.

From its founding, the United States was a settler slaving nation, and the ownership of human beings and Native genocide were central concerns at its 1787 Constitutional Convention. At its first meeting as an independent nation, two key policies were debated and implemented, mandating African slavery and Native genocide. The first was Article 1 of the US Constitution, which counted African slaves as three-fifths of a person when counting state populations—a "compromise" that bolstered the political power of slave states and exempted Indians from counting as part of state populations, since they were not citizens and were not taxed. The second was the Northwest Ordinance, which annexed the Ohio River and Great Lakes regions, nearly doubling the territory of the United States by carving up Native land for white settlement and barring new states from becoming slave states, while allowing for the capture of "fugitive" African people. According to the ordinance, Native people "shall never be invaded or disturbed, unless in just and lawful wars authorized by Congress." In other words, if land cessions could not be achieved through treaty, genocidal war could be waged. Cooperate with the United States or face its wrath; this became the guiding principle for Indian policy.

These two touchstone policies kept in place and expanded slavery, even in so-called "free states," where runaway African people still faced capture. They also formalized genocidal Native wars to take the land and to expand the institution of slavery further westward. Every time a new settler state was added to the union—cut from Native flesh, blood, and soil—settlers fought each other over whether or not the addition would be a slave state, or states were added to keep the balance of so-called "free states."

Early nineteenth-century Indian policy coincided with the expansion of slavery and white supremacy. For example, while the so-called "Five Civilized Tribes"—the Cherokees, Choctaws, Chickasaws, Creeks, and Seminoles—each participated in the enslavement of Africans and the southern plantation economy, each was also targeted for removal west of the Mississippi River to clear the land of Native peoples to make way for a white-dominated slave economy. An 1831 US Supreme Court decision justifying the removal of eastern Native nations also defined Native peoples as "domestic dependent nations" with ever-diminishing rights and territory. In other words, Native peoples were wards of the government, legally infantilized and not fully sovereign or human, and they remain so under current federal Indian law.

After formal emancipation following the Civil War and the abolition of treaty-making in 1871, the settler state shifted tactics, implementing Jim Crow segregation in the South and assimilation policies to "kill the Indian, save the man" through the boarding school system and the Dawes Allotment Act of 1887, which aimed to transfer millions of acres of collectively held Native land into individual hands. This opened the way for white settlement of remaining "surplus" lands. Once reservations had served their purpose as open-air concentration camps, the next project was to imprison Native children in boarding schools, where thousands disappeared and died; those who did survive were scarred for life by the rampant sexual, physical, and psychological violence they experienced at the hands of nuns, priests, and schoolteachers.

The Canton Insane Asylum for Indians in South Dakota was also a carceral institution where gender nonconforming and queer people and those endowed with spiritual powers were sent in an attempt to eliminate alternative sexualities—other political orders—that offended the heteronormative settler body politic. Nine of every ten Native "patients" imprisoned at Canton died there, making it a site of sustained genocide until its closing. The goal of the boarding school and the asylum was to remove Native people from the land and their nations and to eliminate relations among Native peoples and their lands. The first step was to criminalize them to justify their perpetual state of wardship and imprisonment.

Following the mass revolts around the world and colonized peoples clamoring for independence following World War II, the United States led a violent crackdown on revolutionary organizations. The FBI's COINTELPRO program aimed to crush and discredit the Communist Party, and later the Black Panther Party and the American Indian Movement. In 1969, American Indian activists occupied Alcatraz Island, site of a former federal prison that once imprisoned Hopis who had refused to send their children to boarding schools. This time, however, American Indian activists hoped to turn the notorious prison into an "all-Indian University" for North American Native culture, history, and freedom. Afterward, the Red Power Movement took the continent by storm. The movement dovetailed with, and drew inspiration from, the Black Freedom Movement, which turned its attention to ending police violence and incarceration by demanding jobs and resources for schools and health care. What they got instead was more prisons and more police. Once again, as was the case with slavery, labor and time were the key aspects of incarceration, which means the theft of both, the theft of life.

The prison population grew exponentially from two hundred thousand inmates in the late 1960s to 2.4 million inmates in the 2000s, mostly targeting Black and Native people, people of color, and the poor. This was a response to the growing revolutionary militancy of Black and Native movements. In other words, prisons are an instrument of class rule, and, therefore, colonial rule. Instead of upholding treaties and equality, prisons mediate the crisis of Native and Black lives. They aim to crush the visions of freedom—the worlds that could have been and still could be—in North America, beginning with the first slave revolt, in 1527, at San Miguel de Guadalupe, which freed African people and Native land from European rule.

While abolition has been a key feature of the Black Freedom Movement, it also resonates with Native struggles. "Freedom is a place," Ruth Wilson Gilmore states when speaking of abolition geography.[1] Anti-Blackness, Native elimination, and white supremacy are baked into the history of the United States, and you cannot un-bake a cake. Therefore, decolonization means the unequivocal abolition of prisons and police, the caretakers of violence and the gendarmes of capitalism, for the land and the people of North America to be free.

Kinship

Kinship is a term popularized by one of the founding fathers of American anthropology, Lewis Henry Morgan. Morgan made a name for himself in the latter half of the nineteenth century by studying Haudenosaunee social organization. It was from these studies that he developed his theory of kinship. Unlike many of his contemporaries who saw Native people as subhuman and deserving of genocide, Morgan saw Indians as savages in need of salvation. He developed sympathy for Indian rights and used his research to advocate for the humane integration of Native people into American society, working closely with the US government to achieve this goal. Today, Native scholars call Morgan's approach the "white savior" complex, which is just as racist as the ideas of his anti-Indian contemporaries who sought the outright elimination of Native people.

Given the anti-Indian roots of settler anthropology, the term *kinship* is perhaps not well-suited for describing Native experience or politics. However, the attributes of Haudenosaunee kinship that Morgan identified—personal dignity, equality, freedom and autonomy, fraternity, matriarchy, and the absence of poverty—remain central to contemporary Native social relations and political projects, regardless of how Morgan attempted to use Native kinship to normalize settler colonialism. This is because Native kinship relations are still alive and strong, if not always in practice, then in the imagination of Native revolutionaries seeking to end the exploitation, extraction, and dispossession of Native life that drives the moral economy of bordertowns.

What does kinship look like as a form of politics? One need look no further than the circles of support that Native transwomen have developed to keep their sisters safe in the informal and often predatory economies of sex work that are common in bordertowns. One need look no further than the gangs of unsheltered Native people, often intergenerational and multi-gendered, who watch out for one another when confronted with violence from police, business owners, or predators on the streets. One need look no further than the solidarity meals and supply drives that grassroots Native organizations conduct to care for poor and unsheltered Native relatives in bordertowns. All of these acts of Native kinship are political, because they defy the narrative of alienation and loss that is commonly used to describe urban Native life. This narrative presumes that Native people are dying, culturally and physically. The proliferation of kinship in contemporary Native environmental justice struggles and everyday life tells a different story, a story of strength and hope. Native traditions of kinship can be forged anywhere, and the bonds that tie us together can be made and remade to protect all our relations, human and otherwise. This act of multispecies protection is an essential expression of Native kinship. It also forms the basis of Native projects for liberation from colonialism, whether these arise from organized resistance against the state or organic refusal of dehumanization by everyday Native people.

It is important, however, to distinguish between kinship and charity. Bordertowns are riddled with churches that use food and services to recruit poor and unsheltered Native people. Churches often subject Native people to sermons as a condition of receiving food. Like loansharks and pawnbrokers, missionaries are predators in bordertowns, using the language of charity and sympathy to prey on poor Native people. They are to the twenty-first century what Lewis Henry Morgan was to the nineteenth: white saviors trading in the souls of savages. The end goal? To convert Native people once and for all to the gospel of US settler capitalism. Bordertown dynamics teach us an important lesson: kinship liberates, charity subjugates.

Solidarity/Alliance

The word *solidarity* is used frequently to describe a relationship of support between people from different backgrounds premised on a shared goal for advancing social and/or environmental justice. There are two types of solidarity. The first is vertical, which typically happens when a person or group with greater class, racial, or gendered privilege leverages their privilege to assist a group with lesser class, racial, or gendered privilege—an oppressed group—with demands for a more humane and just life. Typically, a statement or gesture of solidarity comes with specific pledges of material and political support from the privileged group, whether these pledges involve sending resources to a frontline of struggle or leveraging media, legal, or political influence to assist with a cause. When invoked in the name of progressive causes, statements and gestures of solidarity often involve denouncing certain actions, groups, or tendencies like racism, politicians, police violence, or state repression. To be in solidarity means to leverage one's resources for the greater cause of equality, rights, liberation, and reparations to historically oppressed or colonized groups.

A term and practice related to solidarity is *alliance*. You often hear progressives call on "allies" to assist them in moments of material and political need. Calls for allies typically come from oppressed and colonized groups who need support to win important gains in their struggles for dignity and freedom. Those who commonly answer these calls are well-meaning (often white) individuals and organizations who may or may not know much about the cause or the community issuing the call but, nevertheless, feel compelled to offer support. This leads to a series of difficult contradictions when it comes to allyship. Many Native activists are critical of allyship, because it often functions as a salve for "white guilt" or simply reinforces the "white savior" complex, which we discussed above when addressing charity. Many critics also see allies as willing to pay lip service but unwilling to walk their talk by taking substantial steps to relinquish their own privilege or redistribute their wealth. Those who conduct charity work for Native people, mainly churches and nonprofits, often fall into this category of criticism, because they see oppressed and colonized peoples as wretches in need of salvation. For these types of allies, support isn't motivated by political values; it's simply about helping people. In other words, those who enter into a relationship of solidarity and alliance with an oppressed or colonized group may hold sympathetic views and offer important resources and support, but they do not necessarily possess the political development, or "wokeness," that would allow for full, long-term alignment with more radical demands associated with social and environmental justice. And their solidarity or alliance with these groups typically does not translate into a dramatic reversal of their own social location, which keeps the inequalities (and, therefore, the system of oppression) between those calling for solidarity/alliance and those answering these calls intact. Some have gone so far as to call for disposing of "allies" to make way for "accomplices," which implies stricter criteria for who engages in allyship and more extreme measures for accountability.

The second type of solidarity is lateral between oppressed and colonized groups, as is the case when Native organizations draft statements of solidarity with Palestinian, Black, migrant, or LGBTQI2S causes. The histories of lateral solidarity between oppressed and colonized groups are rich, creating the conditions for some of the most vibrant liberation struggles in human history. These histories often transpire between movements and nations in the Global South that support each other's revolutions in order to make stronger gains.

The primary difference between vertical solidarity and lateral solidarity is the focus: the first is on mutual support between struggles to build the power and capacity of large-scale liberation movements, especially in contexts where the petit bourgeoise and ruling class cannot be trusted or entreated to support these movements, because these movements are advancing a full revolutionary program to overthrow class hierarchy. The second type of solidarity focuses on asking (sometimes begging) for resources and concessions from petit bourgeois and ruling-class individuals like celebrities, philanthropists, politicians, and academics. Movements and causes that invite this latter type of solidarity tend to be temporary, small, single-issue-oriented, and nonrevolutionary; meaning, they tend to focus on reform or small-scale gains without addressing or attacking structural issues like capitalism or settler colonialism. Activists, including Native folks, in the Global North—particularly the United States and Canada—focus most of their energies on practicing and perfecting vertical solidarity. Instead of reproducing the practice of vertical solidarity—which simply reproduces the class contradictions at the heart of this form of solidarity—we believe that any project for Native liberation must emphasize, build, and practice lateral solidarity as its primary form of relationship-making. While vertical solidarity is useful in terms of funneling resources into Native liberation struggles, it should be secondary to lateral solidarity and employed tactically only to assist with specific campaigns.

Land

Native peoples throughout the Western Hemisphere have their own creation narratives about their origins, how their ancestors came to the land as place, and how places are imbued with relationships between other than human beings and beings that became human. The original stories of how Native people came to the land are told through emergence from lower worlds into new worlds or through relationships between humans and holy beings from the Sky and the Earth. Today, this knowledge of our origins, of how to live properly, lies within our respective epistemologies and continues to be conveyed not only through ceremonies and prayer but also through acts of resistance to ongoing Native dispossession.

Since their first appearances in what they called the "New World," waves of European settlers, and then Americans, have been devoted to wresting land and its resources from Native peoples to sustain settler life. Patrick Wolfe argues that "Land is life—or, at least, land is necessary for life. Thus, contests for land can be—indeed, often are—contests for life."[2] Targeted for elimination because of their status as the original peoples who lived on and with the land, Native people were eliminated as "Indians," while enslaved Africans were targeted for elimination for their labor. As Deborah Bird Rose points out, all Native people had to do to be in the way of settler colonization was to stay home.[3]

The shift in the way land is conceived of, even by Native peoples, is through capitalism, which regards land as property. Capitalism organized around the private ownership of the means of production (land, resources, capital) and the private control of the wealth produced by wage laborers became the means through which Native peoples were dispossessed of approximately 97 percent of land in the current United States. By the late nineteenth century and into the early twentieth century, Native people had been removed onto small tracts of land deemed wastelands by settlers. The 97 percent of remaining lands outside of these "reservations" were developed into bordertowns, which carried with them all the legal, social, and spatial fictions that made these lands alien and hostile to Indians who happened to wander "off the reservation."

In the 1950s, as part of termination, Native peoples were relocated to urban spaces as a means of disappearing them from the land once again. Those who were relocated were labeled "strangers in town," another iteration of "off the reservation." Ongoing movements for decolonization center on a commitment to land return. Native people are actively building these movements in the present, renewing kinship ties with the land, water, and all land-based beings to advance the struggle for Native liberation (as seen at Standing Rock, for instance).

LGBTQI2S

The acronym LGBTQI2S—Lesbian, Gay, Bi-Sexual, Transgender, Queer, Intersex, and Two-Spirit—refers to a diversity of gender identities and sexualities that defy the normative gender binary of female and male and the heterosexuality that accompanies it. The term *Two-Spirit*, in particular, acknowledges the cultural distinctiveness of those Native peoples who refuse an identity or sexuality associated with heterosexuality. Rather,

Two-Spirits declare that they are of both the feminine and masculine spirits, making them Two-Spirit.

Native feminisms and queer critiques take up gender studies in a number of ways, including tracing gender diversity in Native societies prior to cycles of colonial invasions, making connections between the presence of LGBTQI2S today and in the past. These studies describe the gender diversity of precontact societies that challenges notions of heterosexual normativity. As unearthed by scholars who engage with and write about queer activists and community organizers prior to settler colonialism, many Native peoples recognized and respected their relatives who did not fit gender binaries. Rather, Native traditional stories and practices of kin relations offer evidence for the presence of female, male, intersex, and multiple genders beyond a third gender, or Two-Spirit. Gender roles within families and societies included nonbinary relatives, and those who did not fall into binary gender roles were valued members of Native societies, even crucial to the survival of people and communities.

Violent colonial invasions displaced Native peoples from their lands and imposed white settler values and practices that sought to destroy traditional kin networks, particularly those that acknowledged multiple genders. As Qwo-Li Driskill argues, violent colonial practices wreaked havoc on Native peoples' ways of being, their connections and claims to land and to each other in ways that have erased how people relate to each other as family and in intimate and sexual relationships.[4] The erasure of Native peoples' ways of being have included colonial insistence that Native peoples transform their sexual and family practices so that the gender binary of the feminine and masculine, rooted especially in the nuclear family unit, becomes the primary category of practicing relationships.

This violent transformation has had many effects, chief among them the elevation and valorization of heteropatriarchy and relations of dominance and subordination based on settler claims of gender as a binary. LGBTQI2S activism and organizing unsettle assumptions about the naturalness of the gender binary, work to recover the presence of multiple genders in Native societies, and map how the forces of white settler colonialism have transformed Native nations and peoples into heterosexual normativity. As Joanne Barker asserts, conversations about Native rights must include LGBTQI2S issues and concerns, for all of our relations must be included in Native rights and responsibilities as Native peoples assert their claims against imperialist and colonialist state formations in the United States and Canada.

Sovereignty

Perhaps one of the most infamous and absurd definitions of sovereignty comes from former US president George W. Bush who, when asked by a journalist about the sovereignty of Native nations, said, "Tribal sovereignty means that. It's sovereign. You're . . . you're a . . . you've been given sovereignty and you're viewed as a sovereign entity."[5] Bush's response to the question might not enlighten the public, because they are generally ignorant about the Native presence within the US; however, Native peoples were not surprised, because they live within a settler nation whose existence is founded on the theft of an entire continent and its resources and dedicated to Native elimination, while simultaneously stealing Black labor to continually remake its empire.

On the one hand, Native leaders, scholars, and community people assert sovereignty as the inherent authority of Native peoples to govern themselves as the first peoples of the continent, and, on the other hand, Native peoples find themselves reduced to "wards" of the United States, which holds Native lands in a "trust" relationship, with Native nations cast as "domestic dependents" of the United States. The historical and legal process through which Native nations became "domestic dependents" of the United States is traced to the Marshall Trilogy, Supreme Court Justice John Marshall's legal opinions that established the doctrinal basis for interpreting federal Indian law and defining tribal sovereignty. Three cases, *Johnson v. McIntosh*, *Cherokee Nation v. Georgia*, and *Worcester v. Georgia*, effectively circumvented Native sovereignty so that today Native nations find themselves straitjacketed in multiple ways that include the loss of their water rights and an inability to build sustainable infrastructures on their lands or establish any kind of meaningful institutions that will fully benefit their citizens. As wards of the federal government, Native peoples are cast into racial categories and named as another "minority," thereby rendering them as no different than any other person who either immigrated to this land, is a descendant of immigrants, or whose ancestors came to this land as enslaved people. Native peoples continually assert that they are not part of any multicultural racial minority. As the original peoples of this land, they have a distinct relationship to the land, the natural world, and all nonhuman beings. This relationship is *manifested in their epistemologies* in such a way that defies the category of a racial minority.

Taking into account what "sovereignty" means on Native peoples' terms is an ongoing process that acknowledges histories entangled with settler colonialism that have profoundly transformed Native nations and nationalisms, often in ways that reinscribe settler values that practice forms of discrimination across race, gender, and class. Native peoples acknowledge the fraught history of nation-building and citizenship as it is now practiced within their own governing structures and communities. Native peoples strive to assert a sovereignty based on their original kinship to land, communities, and each other.

Decolonization

Decolonization is a diverse political and intellectual tradition with multiple iterations and origins. Revolutionaries from around the world have struggled—sometimes successfully—for decolonization. Historically speaking, decolonization is linked to the emergence of Third World politics, which came after World War II, when colonized peoples rose up to struggle for national liberation from imperial and colonial control by European nations like Great Britain, Portugal, Spain, Belgium, and France. Decolonization has a shorter history in the Global North—namely Canada and the United States—where it is often linked with the struggles of Native people to maintain and reclaim traditional practices. Often, decolonization in this context centers on overcoming colonialism by healing and returning to traditional ideas of identity, governance, and land-based relationality. It is also sometimes associated with land repatriation. Less often, decolonization is envisioned as overthrowing the fundamental coloniality that defines the relationship between settler states and Native nations, which would effectively mean the demise of settler states and the restoration of Native sovereignty premised on values of caretaking, democracy, equality, and autonomy.

During the 1970s, organizations like the Coalition for Navajo Liberation, Indians Against Exploitation, and the American Indian Movement advanced decolonization in bordertowns to challenge rampant anti-Indian racism from white citizens, business owners, politicians, and police. This generation of Native revolutionaries demanded redress for these wrongs through the strengthening of Indian civil rights and economic equality. They were part of a generation that demanded crucial laws to protect Native people from the anti-Indian racism that fuels settler colonialism.

Because we have not effectively overthrown settler colonialism, anti-Indian racism remains a fundamental practice in bordertowns and, indeed, everywhere. The decolonization of bordertowns must, therefore, continue to tackle these same issues. This is why we must be wary of certain forms of redress and justice that are recommended under the banner of decolonization. For example, some would have us believe that decolonization is best achieved through healing and reconciliation with everyday purveyors of anti-Indianism: settler citizens, business owners, politicians, and police. This is the Trojan Horse version of decolonization that smuggles in everything inherent to colonization, while changing nothing. It relies on the idea that colonization is just a state of mind rather than a violent structure. These advocates argue that if we change the minds and hearts of our oppressors—if we teach cops to be more sensitive about Native culture; if we form Indian commissions to remind politicians that Native people are human beings; if we commit ourselves to nonviolence and peace—then the violence will end. They claim that all we need to do is formulate a shared path, to build bridges toward reconciliation with settlers and live in peaceful coexistence. These are all liberal versions of decolonization that conform with settler colonialism's version of reconciliation. No one is held responsible and the structure remains intact.

The question of responsibility is fundamentally a question of justice. And the question of justice is at the center of decolonization. How can we reconcile with a system that refuses our calls for justice? How can we make peace with a structure that remains hell-bent on our destruction? It is unethical and irresponsible to advance a politics that presumes reconciliation will somehow magically translate into peace for everyone. In a world structured by the elimination of Native peoples, peace—which is the ideal outcome of all forms of justice—can only be achieved through collective struggle to abolish settler colonialism and hold its most pernicious agents responsible. Anything short of this is a form of pacification that places a feel-good salve on colonization without confronting the intractability of the system and its fundamental reliance on anti-Indianism (in other words, violence). Those who advocate for decolonization must not be afraid to engage the material conditions of colonialism and decolonization, however uncomfortable or unsettling this may be to their liberal sensibilities. Liberalism upholds settler colonialism. In its final formulation, it cannot offer any meaningful or transformative forms of justice for the wrongs of colonialism. We are capable of and responsible for defining justice ourselves. This must be the basis of our decolonial praxis.

Liberation

In the summer of 1974, the Coalition for Navajo Liberation (CFNL) descended on the bordertown of Farmington, New Mexico, to protest anti-Navajo racism and discrimination from white townspeople and vigilantes in the wake of the Chokecherry Massacre. An article about this uprising appeared that August in the *New York Times*. The article's author, Martin Waldron, interviewed Wilbert Tsosie, a CFNL member. "We are nothing more than dirt," Tsosie explained, "They have played with us, killed us, destroyed us—in alleys, restaurants, jails and bars." Waldron framed Tsosie's comments and the CFNL's motivation as a "yearning for revenge" for this treatment.[6]

Waldron was a well-respected and prominent journalist at the *New York Times* who had previously won a Pulitzer Prize for his reporting. He was, thus, clearly held in high regard. Framing the CFNL's agenda as a yearning for revenge was likely accepted as the correct way to interpret the politics of liberation advocated by the group. The Diné youth who founded the group chose the term *liberation* purposefully to describe their politics and their goal. Did they, as Waldron claims, equate liberation with revenge?

The root of *liberation* is *liberate*, which means to free or to emancipate. But to free from what? Historically, the term *liberation* has been used by advocates to end slavery or other institutions of oppression. Women's liberation, for example, has long sought to free women from patriarchal oppression. Following the Russian Revolution, the Marxist term *national liberation* became a vehicle for revolutionary movements in the Third World to remove imperial powers like Great Britain, France, Portugal, Belgium, and others from their lands and establish national self-determination. In other words, Third World movements for self-determination sought liberation from the oppressive foreign imperial powers that occupied their lands and controlled their people through force. This type of foreign imperialism practiced by European nations was also called *colonialism*, because imperial powers turned large swaths of land and peoples in Africa, Asia, and Latin America into colonies, which they ruled through coercive and oppressive practices. Therefore, national liberation during this period was tied closely to decolonization, because the removal of European imperial control in the colonies required the overthrow and dismantling of local colonial structures and the emergence of Third World nationalism.

It is a common misperception to see the history of Native people in the United States as a history of racial oppression alone, or even a history first and foremost of resistance to colonialism. Native nations were the first nations to encounter, challenge, and resist the imperialism of the so-called New World, an imperialism emanating not from Europe but from the new nation called the United States. Seeking to consolidate itself "from sea to shining sea," the US government waged an all-out imperial war against Native nations, murdering them through genocidal campaigns, removing them from land through scorched earth campaigns, and eventually subjugating them through law (the Marshall Trilogy is the clearest example). While this was obviously a project of settler colonialism, it was also a project of imperialism. Evidence for this claim can be found in how the US government labels Native resistance. From the onset of US westward expansion, Native resistance forces organized by iconic figures like Sitting Bull, Geronimo, and Crazy Horse were called enemies of the state. To this day, any nation or force that resists US foreign expansion into its lands, including locations in the Middle East, Latin America, and the Pacific, is labeled an enemy of the United States—terrorist. As previously mentioned, this is why the 2011 capture and murder of Osama bin Laden was called "Operation Geronimo" by the US government. Native people who resisted US expansion and refused colonial subjugation were the first enemies of the state—the original terrorists.

Native liberation, then, is a struggle by Native people to free themselves from the oppressive colonial and imperial authority of the United States. While this has required many forms of resistance, it has also required a commitment to liberation; Native people have not only acted *against* US imperialism and colonialism through resistance, they have also *advocated for* an alternative future through decolonization and liberation. This is partly why we use the language of self-determination and sovereignty to describe our rights as nations. Our vision of the future means having the freedom to make decisions for ourselves without interference from the US government. Because the United States uses settler colonialism to perpetuate its imperial subjugation of Native nations, Native liberation must also be a struggle for decolonization. Liberation, in the parlance of the CFNL, as well as later Red Power iterations like The Red Nation, is, therefore, an anti-imperialist and anti-colonial struggle that seeks to build a more just world in which Native people and all life are free.

When we speak of liberation as Native people, we do not mean revenge. Revenge is a simplistic, ahistorical, and apolitical understanding of what motivates Native action. Given that Waldron was a white settler journalist based on the East Coast, it's fair to assume he possessed little knowledge about Native politics or colonialism. And this general ignorance likely led him to reduce the CFNL's intentions to a mere act of revenge, as if the young Diné members of this group were nothing more than murderous savages foaming at the mouth and trying to topple white civilization (which, of course, is also a racist trope used to demean Native people and justify the classification of Native resistance to US imperialism as a form of terrorism). No, when we speak of liberation, we mean a desire to be free—once and for all—from the imposition of the United States on our lands, affairs, bodies, minds, spirits, and cultures.

CHAPTER EIGHT

Don't Go Back to the Reservation: A Bordertown Manifesto

I. The future is Native.

We are exiles from a Native future no longer governed by the logic of the bordertown. The kinship relations we enact in the present are the seeds of a blossoming Native liberation. The bordertown, and, thus, settler colonialism, stands no chance against Native kinship, capacious in its just relations with non-Native people and other than human relations. Ours is a kinship built for the future, because it is a kinship that survived the past. Ours is a kinship that made and continues to make alliances with the enemies of settler order: migrant, Black, and refugee relatives, women and queer relatives, and the darker nations of the Global South whose presence, like ours, threatens settler order.

We are locked in a fight with settlers whose viciousness and savagery compensate for the precarity their presence makes in lands that do not claim them. This is their kinship. We have burned their villages to the ground before to protect our lands and nations. We will do it again to liberate our relatives. These will not be fires of destruction but of creation and reclamation. Only in the ashes of the bordertown will we find the raw material for our liberation. In the name of Native kinship, we will redistribute stolen land and stolen wealth hoarded in their bordertowns, and this will create an abundance and equality for all life. Settler colonialism and capitalism interrupted Native kinship. When settlers are gone, we will resume this kinship as a practice and a place.

II. All land is Native, and all settler towns and cities are bordertowns.

There is no "rural" or "urban," no "rez" or "city"; there is only the border-town. The border exists everywhere settler order confronts Native order. Everything in a settler world is a border. Our persistent survival is the primary contradiction and the unresolvable crisis of settler colonialism. Settlers enforce the logic of bordertowns to overcome this contradiction. This is their primary job and the essence of their existence as settlers. They are born vigilantes in the making, taught to fear Native people and to see Native society as a threat. These are the conditions that give life to the violence of settler society. The Indian must be eliminated for no other reason than that we represent an alternative political order, one that precedes settler society and that holds within it the destruction of settler reality.

III. The values that govern life in all settler nations—competition, aggression, self-interest, exclusion, violence, exploitation—are values learned, practiced, and perfected in the bordertown.

The bordertown is the violent wellspring from which all of settler society is made and remade. Settlers flew flags made of the scalps of our murdered ancestors over their forts, those outposts of early British, French, Spanish, and American imperialism. These were all bordertowns. Plymouth and Jamestown were bordertowns. The frontier man camps and settlements built to facilitate colonial, capitalist exploitation like mining, fracking, logging, ranching, and commercial hunting were bordertowns. All settler cities and towns were born as bordertowns and, today, maintain the primary characteristic of a bordertown: Native erasure.

IV. Settler colonialism and capitalism go hand in hand.

Bordertowns were the first outposts of capitalist expansion and today represent the culmination of this system. Bordertown economies are designed to feed off Native life in order to capture value for settler society. Bordertowns require the elimination of the Native as the necessary condition for settlers to accumulate wealth and power. Settler colonialism and capitalism go hand in hand in the bordertown.

V. Native death is the raw material that built the bordertown.

Settler society defines settler inclusion through Native exclusion, and the bordertown defines settler life through Native death. It was to the bordertown schools that our stolen children were sent. It has been on our sacred ground, desecrated by bordertown liquor stores and bars, that we find our relatives murdered by settler vigilantes. It is in the arroyos, rivers, and mesas of our ancestral territories that we find the bodies of relatives left to die from exposure. Like a snake, the bordertown's payday loan stores, pawnshops, and trading posts hunt us and seize us in their debt grip. The settler's hospitals treat us like animals. Their churches treat us like heathens. Our deaths give the bordertown life. The bordertown must die for Native people to live.

VI. The bordertown cannot be reformed. Settler society cannot be redeemed.

Like all colonial occupations, settler projects are violent but temporary. There is one inexorable fact of settler society: its demise. Insecurity haunts settler societies. Indians are the nightmare of the settler present. Even as ghosts that haunt street names and sports mascots, we are feared. As metaphors for settler military campaigns we are loathed, for we are the original insurgents who defeated US empire. Settlers are consumed by this fear and loathing. They cannot escape the fact that they are foreigners squatting on borrowed land and living on borrowed time. This is why settlers created "the Second Amendment." It is how settlers constitute violence as the guiding logic and value of all social relations. Their power over the land and its people comes from this violence and threat of violence. Settlers came to stay, but their days are numbered. They grow increasingly violent in their desperation to maintain their occupation of foreign lands. Their Second Amendment will not save them from their future. We are building a liberated society, and there is no place in it for the "settler."

VII. Private property mediates all expressions of settler kinship.

Property is kinship to settlers. Their wealth is extracted from our land and the labor of Africans they enslaved. It is through property that a settler stakes claim to land that will never claim them back. Like bordertowns, property is not natural; it is built from the blood of Native and Black ancestors. Property requires borders to make sense as a form of enclosure. As such, it requires constant violence. Settlers express their identities and their freedoms through property. They worship at the altar of private property. This is why settlers so fiercely protect the relations and conditions (like borders) that make private property possible. Do not let settlers confuse you with their talk about "liberties" and "constitutional rights." This is the bluster of those concerned about one thing only: their "freedom" to dominate, destroy, own, and accumulate property. The bordertown is the laboratory where settler freedom-cum-property is made and remade. Since the erection of the first bordertown, settlers have called it their "duty" to use violence to protect their property. The origins of modern police can be found in militias and patrols whose "duty" it was to recover enslaved Africans (property) and kill Indians to acquire land (which they converted to property). The institution of police is settler kinship in its purest form.

VIII. There is no Native liberation in a heteropatriarchal world.

Bordertowns first appeared as man camps. Man camps always begin as "temporary" settlements for prospectors—mostly white men—to make fast cash on the capitalist frontier of permanent plunder. While man camps often disperse when the boom of speculative economies turns bust, many become bordertowns. Bordertowns are man camps at an advanced stage that hold the same original characteristics of the man camp. Wall Street is an advanced man camp. The White House is a man camp in miniature. The Bakken oil field is an emergent man camp. The Sturgis Motorcycle Rally is an annual man camp. The Ivy League is a federation of man camps. The man camp is where and how settler men establish and renew their identity as conquerors and owners. Of property. Of women. Of the monopoly on violence. The man camp begets settler fraternity born of violence: violence against the land, violence against women, violence against Indians. In bordertowns, settler boys are taught to be settler men through the rituals of Indian killing and woman hating. The logic of the bordertown-cum-man camp spawned Missing and Murdered Native Women and Girls. The only way to achieve liberation is to destroy the man camp.

IX. Settler colonialism is the disease. Decolonization and abolition are the cure.

Under the conditions of a devastating global pandemic, settlers refuse to wear masks. They claim it robs them of their "liberties." They whine because they cannot accumulate property or survey their domain uninterrupted. They protest with guns to demand the right to be served and catered to. This is our present moment, but this has always been true with settlers. The present moment reinforces what we already know: settlers are parasites. They need us—the value they extract and exploit from our labor and land—to survive. We don't need them. We outnumber them. They use diseases like COVID-19 to dwindle our numbers and kill our dreams for liberation, so they can settle back into their version of normal. Settlers are the preexisting condition that plagues us all. Join the mass uprising that demands decolonization and abolition to rid ourselves of the infection of settler colonialism.

X. Native liberation will be won in the bordertown.

There is nothing natural about settler relations, thus, there is nothing natural about the settler. What the settler calls democracy, we call unfreedom. What the settler calls property, we call violence. What the settler takes for granted, we seek to abolish. Abolishing private property liberates land from the borders that imprison it. Bordertown justice envisions a world without borders. We abolish borders by burning bordertowns to the ground. Without borders, capitalism dies. When there are no longer borders, settler colonialism too ceases to exist. When there are no longer borders, we will be free to live in peace and harmony with all our relations.

There is more than one way to kill a settler. Settlers want us to match their guns with ours, because the only language they speak is violence. They are terrified, because they already know the truth, the source of their demise and our power: this land never stopped claiming us. Ours is a language of equality and beauty that comes from our unbroken kinship with the Earth. When we speak of Native liberation as the path toward planetary freedom, we speak of a path that is made and remade each time we give offerings to the land. This is who we have always been as Native people. We need nothing else to chart this path into a new world; our history is our future.

Enclosure violates and scars the land. We must destroy private property to liberate Mother Earth. We will redistribute wealth to all humble people of the Earth from the rubble of private property. We will return Native people to their rightful path of development as nations upholding treaties of peace and harmony with the Earth. There are many ways to do this. But the abolition of private property must be our shared goal if we are to have any hope of a future. Join us in this struggle for liberation.

Notes

Foreword

1   "Albuquerque 'Homeless' Double-Killing Survivor Says Teens Giggled," NBC News, July 21, 2014, accessed August 17, 2020, https://tinyurl.com/y5o3ncv6; see video, 2:39.

Chapter 1

1   Cheryl I. Harris, "Whiteness as Property," *Harvard Law Review* 106, no. 8 (June 1993): 1707–91, accessed August 17, 2020, https://sph.umd.edu/sites/default/files/files/Harris_Whiteness%20as%20Property_106HarvLRev-1.pdf.

2   Paula Gunn Allen, *Going Off the Reservation: Reflections on Boundary-Busting, Border-Crossing Loose Cannons* (Boston: Beacon, 1998), 6.

3   Frederick Jackson Turner, *The Significance of the Frontier in American History* (London: Penguin, 2008 [1893]); for a transcription of the original speech, see "The Significance of the Frontier in American History (1893)," American Historical Association, accessed August 17, 2020, https://tinyurl.com/yahgd6sy.

4   Fernando Santos, "Violent Attacks on Homeless in Albuquerque Expose City's Ills," *New York Times*, July 23, 2014, accessed August 17, 2020, https://tinyurl.com/y6p35cba.

Chapter 2

1   Elizabeth Cook-Lynn, *Anti-Indianism in Modern America: A Voice from Tatekeya's Earth* (Champaign: University of Illinois Press, 2001), x.

2   Antonio Gramsci, *Selections from the Prison Notebooks of Antonio Gramsci*, trans. Quintin Hoare (New York: International Publishers, 1973), 419.

3   Audra Simpson, "Settlement's Secret," *Cultural Anthropology* 26, no. 2 (May 2011): 205–17, accessed August 17, 2020, https://tinyurl.com/y2tcl66s.

4   Patrick Wolfe, "Settler Colonialism and the Elimination of the Native," *Journal of Genocide Research* 8, no. 4 (December 2006): 388, accessed August 17, 2020, https://www.tandfonline.com/doi/full/10.1080/14623520601056240.

5   Jodi Byrd, *The Transit of Empire: Indigenous Critiques of Colonialism* (Minneapolis: University of Minnesota, 2011), xxxv.

6   Arthur V. Watkins, "Termination of Federal Supervision: The Removal of Restrictions over Indian Property and Person," *Annals of the American Academy of Political and Social Science* 311, no. 1 (May 1957): 47–55.

7   Edward Charles Valandra, *Not without Our Consent: Lakota Resistance to Termination, 1950–1959* (Champaign: University of Illinois Press, 2006).

8   Vine Deloria Jr., introduction to Michael L. Lawson, *Dammed Indians Revisited: The Continuing History of the Pick-Sloan Plan and the Missouri River Sioux* (Pierre: South Dakota State Historical Society Press, 2009), xv.

9   Henry Mayhew, *London Labour and the Labour Poor: Those That Will Not Work* (London: Griffin, Bohn, 1861), 1.

10   Russell Means, with Marvin J. Wolf, *Where White Men Fear to Tread: The Autobiography of Russell Means* (Brooklyn: Antenna Books, 1995), 370.

11   Raymond Williams, *Problems in Culture and Materialism* (London: Verso, 1980), 67.

12   Frederick Jackson Turner, *The Significance of the Frontier in American History* (London: Penguin, 2008 [1893]); for a transcription of the original speech, see "The Significance of the Frontier in American History (1893)," American Historical Association, accessed August 17, 2020, https://tinyurl.com/yahgd6sy.

13   Karl Marx, *Capital: A Critique of Political Economy,* vol. 1, trans. Ben Fowkes (London: Penguin, 1976 [1867]).

14   Roxanne Dunbar-Ortiz, *Indigenous Peoples' History of the United States for Young People*, adapted by Jean Mendoza and Debbie Reese (Boston: Beacon Press, 2019), 207.

15   A Tribe Called Red, "Burn Your Village to the Ground," Soundcloud, accessed August 20, 2020, https://soundcloud.com/a-tribe-called-red/burn-your-village-to-the-ground.

16   *Yazzie/Martinez v. New Mexico*, no. D-101-CV-2014-02224, (NM. FJDCR. 2018), July 20, 2018, accessed August 20, 2020, https://www.maldef.org/assets/pdf/2018-07-20d-101-cv-2014-00793_Decision_and_Order.pdf.

17   Cat Schuknecht, "School District Apologizes for Teacher Who Allegedly Cut Native American Child's Hair," npr, December 6, 2018, accessed August 20, 2020, https://tinyurl.com/yxa32exb.

Chapter 3

1   David Correia, "Indian Killers: Police Violence against Native People in Albuquerque," La Jicarita: An Online Magazine of Environmental Politics in New Mexico, June 8, 2015, accessed August 20, 2020, https://tinyurl.com/y2qxl4zh.

2   Frederick Jackson Turner, *The Significance of the Frontier in American History* (London: Penguin, 2008 [1893]); for a transcription of the original speech, see "The Significance of the Frontier in American History (1893)," American Historical Association, accessed August 17, 2020, https://tinyurl.com/yahgd6sy.

3   Vine Deloria Jr., *Custer Died for Your Sins: An Indian Manifesto* (Norman: University of Oklahoma Press, 1988 [1969]), 78.

4   Ibid., 81.

5   Deborah A. Miranda, "Extermination of the Joyas: Gendercide in Spanish California," *GLQ: A Journal of Lesbian and Gay Studies* 16, nos. 1–2 (April 2010): 253–84.

6   Leanne Betasamosake Simpson, *As We Have Always Done: Indigenous Freedom through Radical Resistance* (Minneapolis: University of Minnesota Press, 2017).

7   Jeremy Pawloski, "No Policy on Hiring Felons," *Albuquerque Journal*, November 30, 2005, accessed August 20, 2020, https://www.abqjournal.com/news/state/412231nm11-30-05.htm

8   To' Kee Skuy' Soo New-wo-Chek', *I Will See You Again: Year 1 Project Report on Missing and Murdered Indigenous Women, Girls, and Two Spirit People of Northern California*, July 2020, 11–14, accessed August 20, 2020, https://tinyurl.com/yyaa7h8j; also see Sovereign Bodies Institute for Reports and Resources on MMIWG2S, accessed August 20, 2020, https://www.sovereign-bodies.org/reports.

9   "Missing and Murdered Indigenous Women and Girls," Urban Indian Health Institute, accessed August 20, 2020, https://www.uihi.org/resources/missing-and-murdered-indigenous-women-girls.

10   Audra Simpson, *Mohawk Interruptus: Political Life across the Borders of Settler States* (Durham, NC: Duke University Press, 2014).

11   "Albuquerque 'Homeless' Double-Killing Survivor Says Teens Giggled," NBC News, July 21, 2014, accessed August 17, 2020, https://tinyurl.com/y503ncv6; see video, 2:39.

12   Ollie Reed Jr., "No Public Health Department in New Mexico in 1918," *Albuquerque Journal*, March 22, 2020, A-1, A4, A5.

13   Keeanga-Yamahtta Taylor, "How Do We Change America? The Quest to Transform This Country Cannot Be Limited to Challenging Its Brutal Police," *New Yorker*, June 8, 2020, accessed August 20, 2020, https://www.newyorker.com/news/our-columnists/how-do-we-change-america.

14   Andrew Siddons, "The Never-Ending Crisis at the Indian Health Service," *Roll Call*, March 5, 2018, accessed August 20, 2020, https://www.rollcall.com/2018/03/05/the-never-ending-crisis-at-the-indian-health-service.

15   Stephen Zuckerman, Jennifer Haley, Yvette Haley, and Marsh Lillie-Blanton, "Health Service Access, Use, and Insurance Coverage among American Indians/Alaska Natives and Whites: What Role Does the Indian Health Service Play?" *American Journal of Public Health* 94, no. 1 (January 2004): 53–59, accessed August 20, 2020, https://www.ncbi.nlm.nih.gov/pmc/articles/PMC1449826.

Chapter 4

1   Jodi A. Byrd, *The Transit of Empire: Indigenous Critiques of Colonialism* (Minneapolis: University of Minnesota Press, 2011).

2   Joanne Barker, *Native Acts: Law, Recognition, and Cultural Authenticity* (Durham, NC: Duke University Press, 2011), 5.

3   Audra Simpson, *Mohawk Interruptus: Political Life across the Borders of Settler State* (Durham, NC: Duke University Press, 2014), 8.

4   Frantz Fanon, *Wretched of the Earth* (New York: Grove Press, 2004 [1963]), 4.

5   Sherene Razack, *Dying from Improvement: Inquests and Inquiries into Indigenous Deaths in Custody* (Toronto: University of Toronto Press, 2015), 4.

6   Ibid., 6.

7   Amnesty International, *Stolen Sisters: A Human Rights Response to Discrimination and Violence against Indigenous Women in Canada* (2004), accessed August 21, 2020, https://www.amnesty.org/download/Documents/92000/amr200032004en.pdf; Amnesty International, *Maze of Injustice: The Failure to Protect Indigenous*

Women from Sexual Violence in the USA (New York: Amnesty International, 2007), accessed August 21, 2020, https://www.amnestyusa.org/pdfs/mazeofinjustice.pdf.

8   Urban Indian Health Institute, *Missing and Murdered Indigenous Women & Girls: A Snapshot of Data from 71 Urban Cities in the United States* (Seattle: Seattle Health Board, 2017), accessed October 11, 2020, UIHI-Missing-and-Murdered-Indigenous-Women-and-Girls-Report-20191009.pdf.

9   Sarah Deer, *The Beginning and End of Rape: Confronting Sexual Violence in Native America* (Minneapolis: University of Minnesota Press, 2015).

10 Ibid., 13.

11 Ibid., 103–6.

12 "Violence from Extractive Industry 'Man Camps' Endangers Indigenous Women and Children," First Peoples Worldwide: University of Colorado Boulder, January 29, 2020, accessed August 21, 2020, https://tinyurl.com/yyp8qd3s; "New Report Finds Increases of Violence Coincides with Oil Boom," First Peoples Worldwide: University of Colorado Boulder, March 14, 2019, accessed August 21, 2020, https://tinyurl.com/y6rana2q.

13 Joanne Barker, ed., *Critically Sovereign: Indigenous Gender, Sexuality, and Feminist Studies* (Durham, NC: Duke University Press, 2017).

14 Nick Estes, *Our History Is the Future: Standing Rock versus the Dakota Access Pipeline, and the Long Tradition of Indigenous Resistance* (New York: Verso, 2019), 89–131, 201–45; also see Roxanne Dunbar-Ortiz, *Indigenous Peoples' History of the United States for Young People*, adapted by Jean Mendoza and Debbie Reese (Boston: Beacon Press, 2019).

15 *Drink and the Indian* (Washington, DC: Board Temperance of the Methodist Church, 1939), 3.

16 John C. McPhee, *Indians in Non-Indian Communities: A Survey of Living Conditions among Navajo and Hopi Indians Residing in Gallup, New Mexico; Farmington, New Mexico; Cortez, Colorado; Flagstaff, Arizona; Winslow, Arizona; Holbrook, Arizona, Prepared as a Service to the Indians and Their Adopted Communities* (Window Rock Area: United States Indian Service, Welfare-Placement Branch, July 1953).

17 Mark Neocleous, *The Fabrication of Social Order: A Critical Theory of Police Power* (London: Pluto Press, 2000), 6.

18 Karl Marx, *Capital: A Critique of Political Economy,* vol. 1, trans. Ben Fowkes (London: Penguin, 1976 [1867]), 885.

19 Ibid., 899.

20 Neocleous, *The Fabrication of Social Order*, 16.

21 Marx, *Capital*, vol. 1, 719.

22 Ibid.

23 Ibid., 797.

24 Ibid., 796.

25 Ibid., 797.

26 Neocleous, *The Fabrication of Social Order*, 18.

27 Karl Marx and Friedrich Engels, *The Communist Manifesto* (New York: International Publishers, 2014 [1848]), 11.

28 Grégoire Chamayou, *Manhunts: A Philosophical History* (Princeton, NJ: Princeton University Press, 2012), 89.

29   Cedric J. Robinson, *Black Marxism: The Making of the Black Radical Tradition* (Chapel Hill: University of North Carolina Press, 1983).

30   Chamayou, *Manhunts*, 63.

31   Nikhil Pal Singh, "The Whiteness of Police," *American Quarterly* 66, no. 4 (December 2014): 1091–99, accessed September 12, 2020, https://tinyurl.com/yyy56vok.

32   Northwest New Mexico Council of Governments, *McKinley County, New Mexico: Comprehensive Plan Update* (McKinley County, NM: 2012), accessed September 12, 2020, https://www.co.mckinley.nm.us/DocumentCenter/View/949/McKinley-County-Comprehensive-Plan.

33   Andrew Carnegie, *The Gospel of Wealth* (New York: Carnegie Corporation of New York, 2017 [1889]), accessed September 12, 2020, https://tinyurl.com/y2jmbo2o.

Chapter 5

1   Tim Giago, *Children Left Behind: The Dark Legacy of Indian Mission Boarding Schools* (Santa Fe: Clear Light Publishing, 2002).

2   Joyce M. Szabo, *Art from Fort Marion: The Silberman Collection* (Norman: University of Oklahoma Press, 2007).

3   Nick Estes and Aileen Brown, "Where Are the Indigenous Children Who Never Came Home?" *High Country News*, September 25, 2018, accessed September 12, 2020, https://tinyurl.com/y6o5s6md; also see Nick Estes, "The US Stole Generations of Indigenous Children to Open the West," *High Country News*, October 14, 2019, accessed September 12, 2020, https://tinyurl.com/y2eu3auc.

4   Ruth Wilson Gilmore, *Golden Gulag: Prisons, Surplus, Crisis, and Opposition in Globalizing California* (Berkeley: University of California Press, 2007), 28.

5   "The Doctrine of Discovery, 1493: A Spotlight on a Primary Source by Pope Alexander VI," Gilder Lehrman Institute of American History, accessed September 12, 2020, https://www.gilderlehrman.org/content/doctrine-discovery-1493.

6   New Mexico Advisory Committee to the United States Commission on Civil Rights, *The Farmington Report: A Conflict of Cultures,* July 1975, accessed September 12, 2020, https://files.eric.ed.gov/fulltext/ED132236.pdf.

7   New Mexico Advisory Committee to the US Commission of Civil Rights, *The Farmington Report: Civil Rights for Native Americans 30 Years Later*, November 2005, accessed September 12, 2020, https://www.usccr.gov/pubs/docs/122705_FarmingtonReport.pdf.

8   Navajo Nation Human Rights Commission, *Assessing Race Relations between Navajos and Non-Navajos, 2008–2009* (St. Michaels, AZ: Navajo Nation Human Rights Commission, 2010), accessed September 12, 2020, https://tinyurl.com/y64pehu8.

9   Melanie K. Yazzie, "Brutal Violence in Border Towns Linked to Colonization," Indian Country Today Media Network, accessed September 13, 2020, https://tinyurl.com/y69bybhh.

Chapter 6

1   Vine Deloria Jr., *Custer Died for Your Sins: An Indian Manifesto* (Norman: University of Oklahoma Press, 1988 [1969]).

2   Dian Million, *Therapeutic Nations: Healing in an Age of Indigenous Human Rights* (Tucson: University of Arizona Press, 2013).

3   Philip J. Deloria, *Playing Indian* (New Haven, CT: Yale University Press, 1998), 104.
4   John Locke, *Two Treatises of Government* (Cambridge: Cambridge University Press, 1988 [1689]).
5   Deloria Jr., *Custer Died for Your Sins*, 5.
6   "Tradition," Lexico, accessed September 13, 2020, https://www.lexico.com/en/definition/tradition.

Chapter 7

1   Ruth Wilson Gilmore, "Abolition Geography and the Problem of Innocence," in Gaye Theresa Johnson and Alex Lubin, eds., *Futures of Black Radicalism* (New York: Verso, 2017), 252.
2   Patrick Wolfe, "Settler Colonialism and the Elimination of the Native," *Journal of Genocide Research* 8, no. 4 (December 2006): 388, accessed August 17, 2020, https://www.tandfonline.com/doi/full/10.1080/14623520601056240.
3   Deborah Rose Bird, *Hidden Histories: Black Stories from Victoria River Downs, Humbert River and Wave Hill Stations* (Canberra, AU: Aboriginal Studies Press, 1991), 46.
4   Qwo-Li Driskill, "Doubleweaving Two-Spirit Critiques: Building Alliances between Native and Queer Studies," *GLQ: A Journal of Lesbian and Gay Studies* 16, no. 1–2 (April 2010): 69–92, accessed September 14, 2020, https://www.joycerain.com/uploads/2/3/2/0/23207256/___double_weave.pdf.
5   Mark Trahant, with Amy Goodman, "Bush on Native American Issues: Tribal Sovereignty Means That. It's Sovereign" (interview), Democracy Now! August 10, 2004, accessed September 14, 2020, https://www.democracynow.org/2004/8/10/bush_on_native_american_issues_tribal.
6   Martin Waldron, "Top Indian Leader Backs Young Navajos on Rights," *New York Times*, August 30, 1974, accessed September 14, 2020, https://tinyurl.com/y2rmm3bh.

Bibliography

"Albuquerque 'Homeless' Double-Killing Survivor Says Teens Giggled." NBC News, July 21, 2014. Accessed August 17, 2020. https://tinyurl.com/y503ncv6.

Amnesty International. *Maze of Injustice: The Failure to Protect Indigenous Women from Sexual Violence in the USA*. New York: Amnesty International, 2007. Accessed August 21, 2020. https://www.amnestyusa.org/pdfs/mazeofinjustice.pdf.

Amnesty International. *Stolen Sisters: A Human Rights Response to Discrimination and Violence against Indigenous Women in Canada*, October 2004. Accessed August 21, 2020. https://www.amnesty.org/download/Documents/92000/amr200032004en.pdf.

Barker, Joanne, ed. *Critically Sovereign: Indigenous Gender, Sexuality, and Feminist Studies*. Durham, NC: Duke University Press, 2017.

Bird, Deborah Rose. *Hidden Histories: Black Stories from Victoria River Downs, Humbert River and Wave Hill Stations*. Canberra, AU: Aboriginal Studies Press, 1991.

Board Temperance of the Methodist Church. *Drink and the Indian*. 100 Maryland Ave., N.E., Washington, DC, 1939.

Correia, David. "Indian Killers: Police Violence against Native People in Albuquerque." La Jicarita: An Online Magazine of Environmental Politics in New Mexico, June 8, 2015. Accessed August 20, 2020. https://tinyurl.com/y2qxl4zh.

Deloria Jr., Vine. *Custer Died for Your Sins: An Indian Manifesto*. Norman: University of Oklahoma Press 1988 [1969].

"The Doctrine of Discovery, 1493: A Spotlight on a Primary Source by Pope Alexander VI." Gilder Lehrman Institute of American History. Accessed September 12, 2020. https://tinyurl.com/y2qxl4zh.

Locke, John. *Two Treatises of Government*. Cambridge: Cambridge University Press, 1988 [1689].

"McKinley County, New Mexico: Comprehensive Plan Update." McKinley County, New Mexico. Accessed September 12 2020. https://tinyurl.com/yxg2zabv.

Million, Dian. *Therapeutic Nations: Healing in an Age of Indigenous Human Rights*. Tucson: University of Arizona Press, 2013.

"Remarks by President Trump, Vice President Pence, and Members of the Coronavirus Task Force in Press Conference." Whitehouse.gov, March 13, 2020. Accessed August 20, 2020. https://tinyurl.com/y6e6yq6d.

Schuknecht, Cat. "School District Apologizes for Teacher Who Allegedly Cut Native American Child's Hair." npr, December 6, 2018. Accessed August 20, 2020. https://tinyurl.com/yxa32exb.

Siddons, Andrew. "The Never-Ending Crisis at the Indian Health Service." *Roll Call*, March 5, 2018. Accessed August 20, 2020. https://www.rollcall.com/2018/03/05/the-never-ending-crisis-at-the-indian-health-service.

"Tradition." Lexico. Accessed September 13, 2020. https://www.lexico.com/en/definition/tradition.

Waldron, Martin. "Top Indian Leader Backs Young Navajos on Rights." *New York Times*, August 30, 1974. Accessed September 14, 2020. https://tinyurl.com/y2rmm3bh.

Yazzie, Melanie K. "Brutal Violence in Border Towns Linked to Colonization." Indian Country Today Media Network. Accessed September 13, 2020. https://tinyurl.com/y69bybhh.

Yazzie/Martinez v. New Mexico. no. D-101-CV-2014-02224, (NM. FJDCR. 2018), July 20, 2018. Accessed August 20, 2020. https://tinyurl.com/y6r6kvff.

Zuckerman, Stephen, Jennifer Haley, Yvette Haley, and Marsh Lillie-Blanton. "Health Service Access, Use, and Insurance Coverage among American Indians/Alaska Natives and Whites: What Role Does the Indian Health Service Play?" *American Journal of Public Health* 94, no. 1 (January 2004): 53–59. Accessed August 20, 2020. https://www.ncbi.nlm.nih.gov/pmc/articles/PMC1449826.

Index

"Passim" (literally "scattered") indicates intermittent discussion of a topic over a cluster of pages.

About the Authors

Nick Estes (Kul Wicasa) is assistant professor of American Studies at the University of New Mexico. He organizes with The Red Nation, a Native-led leftist organization committed to Native liberation. He is also part of the *Abolition: A Journal of Insurgent Politics* collective. His advocacy and research focus on Native resistance, anticolonialism, abolition, decolonization, and anti-capitalism. He is the author of *Our History Is the Future: Standing Rock versus the Dakota Access Pipeline, and the Long Tradition of Indigenous Resistance* (Verso, 2019).

Melanie K. Yazzie (Diné) is an assistant professor in the Departments of Native American Studies and American Studies at the University of New Mexico. She organizes with The Red Nation, a Native-led leftist organization committed to native liberation. She is lead editor of *Decolonization: Indigeneity, Education & Society*, an international journal committed to public intellectualism and social justice.

Jennifer Nez Denetdale (Diné) is a professor of American Studies at the University of New Mexico. She is a strong advocate for Native peoples and serves as chair of the Navajo Nation Human Rights Commission. She is the author of *Reclaiming Diné History: The Legacies of Navajo Chief Manuelito and Juanita* (University of Arizona Press, 2007).

David Correia is associate professor of American Studies at the University of New Mexico. He organizes with AbolishAPD, a research collective focused on confronting the violence of the Albuquerque Police

Department and committed to the abolition of police as we know it. He is the author of *Properties of Violence: Law and Land Grant Struggle in Northern New Mexico* (University of Georgia Press, 2013), co-author, with Tyler Wall, of *Police: A Field Guide* (Verso, 2018), and co-editor, with Tyler Wall, of *Violent Order: Essays on the Nature of Police* (Haymarket, 2020)

Radmilla Cody is a Grammy nominee, multiple Native American Music Awards winner, forty-sixth Miss Navajo Nation, one of NPR's fifty great voices, a Black History Maker Honoree, and an advocate against domestic abuse and violence. Miss Cody is of the Tla'a'schi'i' (Red Bottom People) clan and is born for the Naahilii (African Americans).

Brandon Benallie is a long-time activist, member of The Red Nation, and a cofounder of the K'é Infoshop in Window Rock, Arizona.

For interviews, book reviews, and other news, see the authors' pages on the PM Press website.

ABOUT PM PRESS

PM Press is an independent, radical publisher of books and media to educate, entertain, and inspire. Founded in 2007 by a small group of people with decades of publishing, media, and organizing experience, PM Press amplifies the voices of radical authors, artists, and activists. Our aim is to deliver bold political ideas and vital stories to all walks of life and arm the dreamers to demand the impossible. We have sold millions of copies of our books, most often one at a time, face to face. We're old enough to know what we're doing and young enough to know what's at stake. Join us to create a better world.

PM Press
PO Box 23912
Oakland, CA 94623
www.pmpress.org

PM Press in Europe
europe@pmpress.org
www.pmpress.org.uk

FRIENDS OF PM PRESS

These are indisputably momentous times—the financial system is melting down globally and the Empire is stumbling. Now more than ever there is a vital need for radical ideas.

In the years since its founding—and on a mere shoestring— PM Press has risen to the formidable challenge of publishing and distributing knowledge and entertainment for the struggles ahead. With over 450 releases to date, we have published an impressive and stimulating array of literature, art, music, politics, and culture. Using every available medium, we've succeeded in connecting those hungry for ideas and information to those putting them into practice.

Friends of PM allows you to directly help impact, amplify, and revitalize the discourse and actions of radical writers, filmmakers, and artists. It provides us with a stable foundation from which we can build upon our early successes and provides a much-needed subsidy for the materials that can't necessarily pay their own way. You can help make that happen—and receive every new title automatically delivered to your door once a month—by joining as a Friend of PM Press. And, we'll throw in a free T-shirt when you sign up.

Here are your options:

- **$30 a month** Get all books and pamphlets plus 50% discount on all webstore purchases

- **$40 a month** Get all PM Press releases (including CDs and DVDs) plus 50% discount on all webstore purchases

- **$100 a month** Superstar—Everything plus PM merchandise, free downloads, and 50% discount on all webstore purchases

For those who can't afford $30 or more a month, we have **Sustainer Rates** at $15, $10, and $5. Sustainers get a free PM Press T-shirt and a 50% discount on all purchases from our website.

Your Visa or Mastercard will be billed once a month, until you tell us to stop. Or until our efforts succeed in bringing the revolution around. Or the financial meltdown of Capital makes plastic redundant. Whichever comes first.

500 Years of Indigenous Resistance

Gord Hill

ISBN: 978-1-60486-106-8
$12.00   96 pages

The history of the colonization of the Americas by Europeans is often portrayed as a mutually beneficial process, in which "civilization" was brought to the Natives, who in return shared their land and cultures. A more critical history might present it as a genocide in which Indigenous peoples were helpless victims, overwhelmed and awed by European military power. In reality, neither of these views is correct.

500 Years of Indigenous Resistance is more than a history of European colonization of the Americas. In this slim volume, Gord Hill chronicles the resistance by Indigenous peoples, which limited and shaped the forms and extent of colonialism. This history encompasses North and South America, the development of nation-states, and the resurgence of Indigenous resistance in the post-WW2 era.

Gord Hill is a member of the Kwakwaka'wakw nation on the Northwest Coast. Writer, artist, and militant, he has been involved in Indigenous resistance, anti-colonial and anti-capitalist movements for many years, often using the pseudonym Zig Zag.

Liberating Sápmi: Indigenous Resistance in Europe's Far North

Gabriel Kuhn

ISBN: 978-1-62963-712-9
$17.00   220 pages

The Sámi, who have inhabited Europe's far north for thousands of years, are often referred to as the continent's "forgotten people." With Sápmi, their traditional homeland, divided between four nation-states—Norway, Sweden, Finland, and Russia—the Sámi have experienced the profound oppression and discrimination that characterize the fate of indigenous people worldwide: their lands have been confiscated, their beliefs and values attacked, their communities and families torn apart. Yet the Sámi have shown incredible resilience, defending their identity and their territories and retaining an important social and ecological voice—even if many, progressives and leftists included, refuse to listen.

Liberating Sápmi is a stunning journey through Sápmi and includes in-depth interviews with Sámi artists, activists, and scholars boldly standing up for the rights of their people. In this beautifully illustrated work, Gabriel Kuhn, author of over a dozen books and our most fascinating interpreter of global social justice movements, aims to raise awareness of the ongoing fight of the Sámi for justice and self-determination. The first accessible English-language introduction to the history of the Sámi people and the first account that focuses on their political resistance, this provocative work gives irrefutable evidence of the important role the Sámi play in the resistance of indigenous people against an economic and political system whose power to destroy all life on earth has reached a scale unprecedented in the history of humanity.

The book contains interviews with Mari Boine, Harald Gaski, Ann-Kristin Håkansson, Aslak Holmberg, Maxida Märak, Stefan Mikaelsson, May-Britt Öhman, Synnøve Persen, Øyvind Ravna, Niillas Somby, Anders Sunna, and Suvi West.

"I'm highly recommending Gabriel Kuhn's book Liberating Sápmi *to anyone seeking to understand the world of today through indigenous eyes. Kuhn concisely and dramatically opens our eyes to little-known Sápmi history, then in the perfect follow-up brings us up to date with a unique collection of interviews with a dozen of today's most brilliant contemporary Sámi voices. Bravo."*
—Buffy Sainte-Marie, Cree, singer-songwriter

*"Comprised largely of interviews with Sámi from a broad range of backgrounds—including artists, academics, and activists—*Liberating Sápmi *provides not only a history of Sámi anticolonial resistance but also unique insights into the Sami social movements that have arisen. The book is well illustrated with maps, photographs, and Sámi art."*
—Gord Hill, Kwakwaka'wakw, author of *500 Years of Indigenous Resistance*

A Line in the Tar Sands: Struggles for Environmental Justice

Edited by Joshua Kahn, Stephen D'Arcy, Tony Weis, Toban Black with a Foreword by Naomi Klein and Bill McKibben

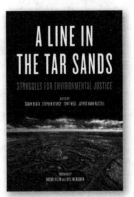

ISBN: 978-1-62963-039-7
$24.95   392 pages

Tar sands "development" comes with an enormous environmental and human cost. In the tar sands of Alberta, the oil industry is using vast quantities of water and natural gas to produce synthetic crude oil, creating drastically high levels of greenhouse gas emissions and air and water pollution. But tar sands opponents—fighting a powerful international industry—are likened to terrorists, government environmental scientists are muzzled, and public hearings are concealed and rushed.

Yet, despite the formidable political and economic power behind the tar sands, many opponents are actively building international networks of resistance, challenging pipeline plans while resisting threats to Indigenous sovereignty and democratic participation. Including leading voices involved in the struggle against the tar sands, *A Line in the Tar Sands* offers a critical analysis of the impact of the tar sands and the challenges opponents face in their efforts to organize effective resistance.

Contributors include: Greg Albo, Sâkihitowin Awâsis, Toban Black, Rae Breaux, Jeremy Brecher, Linda Capato, Jesse Cardinal, Angela V. Carter, Emily Coats, Stephen D'Arcy, Yves Engler, Cherri Foytlin, Sonia Grant, Harjap Grewal, Randolph Haluza-DeLay, Ryan Katz-Rosene, Naomi Klein, Melina Laboucan-Massimo, Winona LaDuke, Crystal Lameman, Christine Leclerc, Kerry Lemon, Matt Leonard, Martin Lukacs, Tyler McCreary, Bill McKibben, Yudith Nieto, Joshua Kahn Russell, Macdonald Stainsby, Clayton Thomas-Muller, Brian Tokar, Dave Vasey, Harsha Walia, Tony Weis, Rex Weyler, Will Wooten, Jess Worth, and Lilian Yap.

The editors' proceeds from this book will be donated to frontline grassroots environmental justice groups and campaigns.

"The tar sands has become a key front in the fight against climate change, and the fight for a better future, and it's hard to overstate the importance of the struggles it has inspired."
—Naomi Klein and Bill McKibben

"Avoiding 'game over for climate' requires drawing a line in the tar sands sludge. A Line in the Tar Sands *makes clear why and how this tar sands quagmire could be the beginning of the end for the mighty fossil fuel industry."*
—Dr. James Hansen, NASA

The Art of Freedom: A Brief History of the Kurdish Liberation Struggle

Havin Guneser with an Introduction by Andrej Grubačić and Interview by Sasha Lilley

ISBN: 978-1-62963-781-5
$15.95   192 pages

The Revolution in Rojava captured the imagination of the Left sparking a worldwide interest in the Kurdish Freedom Movement. *The Art of Freedom* demonstrates that this explosive movement is firmly rooted in several decades of organized struggle.

In 2018, one of the most important spokespersons for the struggle of Kurdish Freedom, Havin Guneser, held three groundbreaking seminars on the historical background and guiding ideology of the movement. Much to the chagrin of career academics, the theoretical foundation of the Kurdish Freedom Movement is far too fluid and dynamic to be neatly stuffed into an ivory-tower filing cabinet. A vital introduction to the Kurdish struggle, *The Art of Freedom* is the first English-language book to deliver a distillation of the ideas and sensibilities that gave rise to the most important political event of the twenty-first century.

The book is broken into three sections: "Critique and Self-Critique: The rise of the Kurdish freedom movement from the rubbles of two world wars" provides an accessible explanation of the origins and theoretical foundation of the movement. "The Rebellion of the Oldest Colony: Jineology—the Science of Women" describes the undercurrents and nuance of the Kurdish women's movement and how they have managed to create the most vibrant and successful feminist movement in the Middle East. "Democratic Confederalism and Democratic Nation: Defense of Society Against Societycide" deals with the attacks on the fabric of society and new concepts beyond national liberation to counter it. Centering on notions of "a shared homeland" and "a nation made up of nations," these rousing ideas find deep international resonation.

Havin Guneser has provided an expansive definition of freedom and democracy and a road map to help usher in a new era of struggle against capitalism, imperialism, and the State.

"Havin Guneser is not just the world's leading authority on the thought of Abdullah Öcalan; she is a profound, sensitive, and challenging revolutionary thinker with a message the world desperately needs to hear."
—David Graeber author of *Debt: The First 500 Years* and *Bullshit Jobs: A Theory*

The Sociology of Freedom: Manifesto of the Democratic Civilization, Volume III

Abdullah Öcalan
with a Foreword by John Holloway
Edited by International Initiative

ISBN: 978-1-62963-710-5
$28.95   480 pages

When scientific socialism, which for many years was implemented by Abdullah Öcalan and the Kurdistan Workers' Party (PKK), became too narrow for his purposes, Öcalan deftly answered the call for a radical redefinition of the social sciences. Writing from his solitary cell in İmralı Prison, Öcalan offered a new and astute analysis of what is happening to the Kurdish people, the Kurdish freedom movement, and future prospects for humanity.

The Sociology of Freedom is the fascinating third volume of a five-volume work titled *The Manifesto of the Democratic Civilization*. The general aim of the two earlier volumes was to clarify what power and capitalist modernity entailed. Here, Öcalan presents his stunningly original thesis of the Democratic Civilization, based on his criticism of Capitalist Modernity.

Ambitious in scope and encyclopedic in execution, *The Sociology of Freedom* is a one-of-a-kind exploration that reveals the remarkable range of one of the Left's most original thinkers with topics such as existence and freedom, nature and philosophy, anarchism and ecology. Öcalan goes back to the origins of human culture to present a penetrating reinterpretation of the basic problems facing the twenty-first century and an examination of their solutions. Öcalan convincingly argues that industrialism, capitalism, and the nation-state cannot be conquered within the narrow confines of a socialist context.

Recognizing the need for more than just a critique, Öcalan has advanced what is the most radical, far-reaching definition of democracy today and argues that a democratic civilization, as an alternative system, already exists but systemic power and knowledge structures, along with a perverse sectarianism, do not allow it to be seen.

The Sociology of Freedom is a truly monumental work that gives profuse evidence of Öcalan's position as one of the most influential thinkers of our day. It deserves the careful attention of anyone seriously interested in constructive thought or the future of the Left.

"Öcalan's works make many intellectuals uncomfortable because they represent a form of thought which is not only inextricable from action, but which directly grapples with the knowledge that it is."
—David Graeber author of *Debt: The First 500 Years*

The Real Cost of Prisons Comix

Ellen Miller-Mack, Craig Gilmore, Lois Ahrens, Susan Willmarth, and Kevin Pyle

ISBN: 978-1-60486-034-4
$14.95   104 pages

Winner of the 2008 PASS Award (Prevention for a Safer Society) from the National Council on Crime and Delinquency

One out of every hundred adults in the U.S. is in prison. This book provides a crash course in what drives mass incarceration, the human and community costs, and how to stop the numbers from going even higher. This volume collects the three comic books published by the Real Cost of Prisons Project. The stories and statistical information in each comic book are thoroughly researched and documented.

Prison Town: Paying the Price tells the story of how the financing and site locations of prisons affects the people of rural communities in which prison are built. It also tells the story of how mass incarceration affects people of urban communities where the majority of incarcerated people come from.

Prisoners of the War on Drugs includes the history of the war on drugs, mandatory minimums, how racism creates harsher sentences for people of color, stories of how the war on drugs works against women, three strikes laws, obstacles to coming home after incarceration, and how mass incarceration destabilizes neighborhoods.

Prisoners of a Hard Life: Women and Their Children includes stories about women trapped by mandatory sentencing and the "costs" of incarceration for women and their families. Also included are alternatives to the present system, a glossary, and footnotes.

Over 125,000 copies of the comic books have been printed and more than 100,000 have been sent to people who are incarcerated, to their families, and to organizers and activists throughout the country. The book includes a chapter with descriptions of how the comix have been put to use in the work of organizers and activists in prison and in the "free world" by ESL teachers, high school teachers, college professors, students, and health care providers throughout the country. The demand for the comix is constant and the ways in which they are being used are inspiring.

"I cannot think of a better way to arouse the public to the cruelties of the prison system than to make this book widely available."
—Howard Zinn

Maroon Comix: Origins and Destinies

Edited by Quincy Saul with illlustrations by Seth Tobocman, Mac McGill, Songe Riddle, and more

ISBN: 978-1-62963-571-2
$15.95   72 pages

Escaping slavery in the Americas, maroons made miracles in the mountains, summoned new societies in the swamps, and forged new freedoms in the forests. They didn't just escape and steal from plantations—they also planted and harvested polycultures. They not only fought slavery but proved its opposite, and for generations they defended it with blood and brilliance.

Maroon Comix is a fire on the mountain where maroon words and images meet to tell stories together. Stories of escape and homecoming, exile and belonging. Stories that converge on the summits of the human spirit, where the most dreadful degradation is overcome by the most daring dignity. Stories of the damned who consecrate their own salvation.

With selections and citations from the writings of Russell Maroon Shoatz, Herbert Aptheker, C.L.R. James, and many more, accompanied by comics and illustrations from Songe Riddle, Mac McGill, Seth Tobocman, and others, *Maroon Comix* is an invitation to never go back, to join hands and hearts across space and time with the maroons and the mountains that await their return.

"*The activist artists of* Maroon Comix *have combined and presented struggles past and present in a vivid, creative, graphic form, pointing a way toward an emancipated future.*"
—Marcus Rediker, coauthor of *The Many-Headed Hydra: Sailors, Slaves, Commoners, and the Hidden History of the Revolutionary Atlantic*

"*With bold graphics and urgent prose,* Maroon Comix *provides a powerful antidote to toxic historical narratives. By showing us what was, Quincy Saul and his talented team allow us to see what's possible.*"
—James Sturm, author of *The Golem's Mighty Swing*

"*The history and stories that the Maroons personified should inspire a whole new generation of abolitionists. This comic illustration can motivate all those looking to resist modern capitalism's twenty-first-century slavery and the neofascism we are facing today.*"
—Dhoruba Bin Wahad, Black Panther Party, New York Chapter, executive director of Community Change Africa

...e in the Whirlwind:
...: Panther 21 to
...:ntury Revolutions

...: Odinga, Dhoruba Bin Wahad,
...:al Joseph
...:dited by Matt Meyer & déqui kioni-sadiki
with a Foreword by Imam Jamil Al-Amin,
and an Afterword by Mumia Abu-Jamal

ISBN: 978-1-62963-389-3
$26.95   648 pages

Amid music festivals and moon landings, the tumultuous year of 1969 included an infamous case in the annals of criminal justice and Black liberation: the New York City Black Panther 21. Though some among the group had hardly even met one another, the 21 were rounded up by the FBI and New York Police Department in an attempt to disrupt and destroy the organization that was attracting young people around the world. Involving charges of conspiracy to commit violent acts, the Panther 21 trial—the longest and most expensive in New York history—revealed the illegal government activities which led to exile, imprisonment on false charges, and assassination of Black liberation leaders. Solidarity for the 21 also extended well beyond "movement" circles and included mainstream publication of their collective autobiography, *Look for Me in the Whirlwind*, which is reprinted here for the first time.

Look for Me in the Whirlwind: From the Panther 21 to 21st-Century Revolutions contains the entire original manuscript, and includes new commentary from surviving members of the 21: Sekou Odinga, Dhoruba Bin Wahad, Jamal Joseph, and Shaba Om. Still-imprisoned Sundiata Acoli, Imam Jamil Al-Amin, and Mumia Abu-Jamal contribute new essays. Never or rarely seen poetry and prose from Afeni Shakur, Kuwasi Balagoon, Ali Bey Hassan, and Michael "Cetewayo" Tabor is included. Early Panther leader and jazz master Bilal Sunni-Ali adds a historical essay and lyrics from his composition "Look for Me in the Whirlwind," and coeditors kioni-sadiki, Meyer, and Panther rank-and-file member Cyril "Bullwhip" Innis Jr. help bring the story up to date.

At a moment when the Movement for Black Lives recites the affirmation that "it is our duty to win," penned by Black Liberation Army (BLA) militant Assata Shakur, those who made up the BLA and worked alongside of Assata are largely unknown. This book—with archival photos from David Fenton, Stephen Shames, and the private collections of the authors— provides essential parts of a hidden and missing-in-action history. Going well beyond the familiar and mythologized nostalgic Panther narrative, *From the Panther 21 to 21st-Century Revolutions* explains how and why the Panther legacy is still relevant and vital today.

Pangayaw and Decolonizing Resistance: Anarchism in the Philippines

Bas Umali

Edited by Gabriel Kuhn

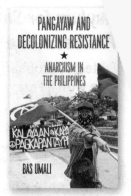

ISBN: 978-1-62963-794-5
Price: $15.00   128 pages

The legacy of anarchist ideas in the Philippines was first brought to the attention of a global audience by Benedict Anderson's book *Under Three Flags: Anarchism and the Anti-Colonial Imagination*. Activist-author Bas Umali proves with stunning evidence that these ideas are still alive in a country that he would like to see replaced by an "archepelagic confederation."

Pangayaw and Decolonizing Resistance: Anarchism in the Philippines is the first-ever book specifically about anarchism in the Philippines. *Pangayaw* refers to indigenous ways of maritime warfare. Bas Umali expertly ties traditional forms of communal life in the archipelago that makes up the Philippine state together with modern-day expressions of antiauthoritarian politics. Umali's essays are deliciously provocative, not just for apologists of the current system, but also for radicals in the Global North who often forget that their political models do not necessarily fit the realities of postcolonial countries.

In weaving together independent research and experiences from grassroots organizing, Umali sketches a way for resistance in the Global South that does not rely on Marxist determinism and Maoist people's armies but the self-empowerment of the masses. His book addresses the crucial questions of liberation: who are the agents and what are the means?

More than a sterile case study, *Pangayaw and Decolonizing Resistance* is the start of a new paradigm and a must-read for those interested in decolonization, anarchism, and social movements of the Global South.

"Isabelo de los Reyes and Mariano Ponce: good men now mostly forgotten even in the Philippines, but crucial nodes in the infinitely complex intercontinental networks that characterize the Age of Early Globalization."
—Benedict Anderson, author of *Under Three Flags: Anarchism and the Anti-Colonial Imagination*

...ale: Profit and
...the Migration Industry

...Siobhán McGuirk & Adrienne
...h a Foreword by Seth M. Holmes

...978-1-62963-782-2
...e: $27.95   368 pages

This explosive new volume brings together a lively cast
of academics, activists, journalists, artists, and people
directly impacted by asylum regimes to explain how
current practices of asylum align with the neoliberal
moment and to present their transformative visions for alternative systems and
processes.

Through essays, artworks, photographs, infographics, and illustrations, *Asylum for
Sale: Profit and Protest in the Migration Industry* regards the global asylum regime as
an industry characterized by profit-making activity: brokers who facilitate border
crossings for a fee; contractors and firms that erect walls, fences, and watchtowers
while lobbying governments for bigger "security" budgets; corporations running
private detention centers and "managing" deportations; private lawyers charging
exorbitant fees; "expert" witnesses; and NGO staff establishing careers while
placing asylum seekers into new regimes of monitored vulnerability.

Asylum for Sale challenges readers to move beyond questions of legal, moral, and
humanitarian obligations that dominate popular debates regarding asylum seekers.
Digging deeper, the authors focus on processes and actors often overlooked in
mainstream analyses and on the trends increasingly rendering asylum available
only to people with financial and cultural capital. Probing every aspect of the
asylum process from crossings to aftermaths, the book provides an in-depth
exploration of complex, international networks, policies, and norms that impact
people seeking asylum around the world. In highlighting protest as well as profit,
Asylum for Sale presents both critical analyses and proposed solutions for resisting
and reshaping current and emerging immigration norms.

"*As the frontiers of disaster capitalism expand, the same systems that drive migration
are finding ever-more harrowing ways to criminalize and exploit the displaced. This
book is part of how we fight back: connecting the extraordinary stories and insights
of people studying, personally navigating, and creatively resisting the global asylum
industry. An unparalleled resource.*"
—Naomi Klein, author of *On Fire: The Burning Case for the Green New Deal*